To Frank and Denise —

In joyous celebration of your marriage

Our love to you —

Amba & Don

THE RULE OF TWO

Observations on Close Relationship

i

Text by Ann Woodin

Drawings by Andrew Rush

Oracle Press, Oracle, Arizona

The Rule of Two

observations on close relationship

Oracle Press
Oracle, Arizona

First Printing
Printed in the United States of America

For our children

Peter
John
Michael
Hugh
Benjamin
Samuel
Joseph
  and
Maggie

By the author:

Home is the Desert
In the Circle of the Sun

About the artist:

Andrew Rush is married to Ann Woodin and is one of the
founding members of Rancho Linda Vista, a community
of the arts, which is the backdrop for this book. He is a
noted draughtsman and a recognized master of the
intaglio print. His work is represented in museums and
collections throughout the world.

Contents

1. The Preamble   1
2. Portraits   21
3. A Portrait Upset   27
4. Upsets   31
5. Maintenance   41
6. Communication   45
7. An Unfinished Conversation   55
8. To Make Oneself Known   63
9. Help and Support   69
10. To Get Off It   73
11. Responsibility   77
12. Commitment   85
13. To Choose   89
14. Contract   93
15. Goals and Purpose   97
16. To Serve   109

Appendixes   113
   I. Additional Portraits of Close Relationship
   II. My Disagreeable Truths
   III. More Questions to Ask Yourself (when you
         sense something is amiss or you
         are upset.)
   IV. My Good Advice
The Afterword (Acknowledgments)   127

1. The Preamble

On my fifth birthday, our cook, whose name was Rose, gave me a red pail and shovel. The following Sunday she took me to my first public beach. As we made our way through the forest of red and blue umbrellas, I held tightly to her hand. I had never seen so many people. Arriving near the water, Rose stopped, "This will do...now you stay close." Then she lay down on the sand and covered her face with a newspaper. After a while, I grew tired of the sand, my new pail and shovel, and turned my attention to a nearby umbrella. Under it lay a man with lots of freckles and beside him knelt a woman in a purple hat. She was smearing some white stuff all over him, and the bracelets on her arms jingled. Every so often she tickled him and he'd laugh and say "Stop that!" But there she'd be, tickling him again. Suddenly he jumped up, grabbed her, slung her over his shoulder like a bag of dog food, and waded out to where the water was deep. She was kicking and laughing and screaming "No, no!" over and over. Then he dropped her with a big splash and her purple hat came off and floated away.

1

All the way home little shivers rippled up my back. I never told
Rose, nor anyone else, what I had seen that day. But that was the
beginning of my interest in relationship, the close human kind. In the
succeeding years, Rose took me on other outings. We went to the park,
to her church, for rides on buses, and once on a train. Wherever we
went, I found a pair of people to look at. And whenever Rose noticed
this, she would say, "Girl, if you stare like that your eyes will fall out."
Or she would say, tugging on my arm, "It's very impolite…so rude." But
how curious people were when close together.

It was as if the whole world were my zoo, and of all the wondrous
and terrible creatures to be seen there, what my eyes kept pursuing
were the 2-headed, 4-legged creatures I later called "relationship": an
old woman with a child, a young man with a woman, two boys, two
girls, a father and son. I was not particular as long as they were close
together. I would look at them and think of the mythical Pushmi-pullyu
Dr. Dolittle discovered on his travels. I would watch one head placidly
chewing its lunch and the other head jawing on and on. I would watch
one pair of eyes observing a bird and the second pair of eyes observing the other's head. I watched hands poking and patting and clasped
behind backs. I watched four legs walking in perfect unison while the
two heads were turned in opposite directions. I stared for hours
(when no one was looking) trying to determine which head was
boss, trying to figure out how this peculiar beast worked. I was, I do
believe, what is called a voyeur.

Even when I married and had children, I still wandered my zoo, still
watching two people together. But as odd as this sounds, I never saw
myself as part of an ordinary, everyday duet, exactly like those which
passed before my eyes. Then I moved to another house, was divorced
and re-married.

Shortly after this event, I stood, one bright morning, shouting (but
not too loudly) at Andy, my new husband. He was tranquilly working at
his desk. "I want to talk to you now! Not later." My eyes were hard as
stones and what I actually wanted to do was hit him. That was far too
scary. So I hit him with words instead. Silence. He did not even look up.
As I gathered my breath to shout again, I heard a small mosquito voice
inside my head. "Well my dear, you can get yourself another husband,

but you can be sure what bothered you with the first will bother you with the second."

The next morning it dawned on me that I was just like every one else, and I had better turn my eyes to the Pushmi-pullyu of which I was a part. But I was not at all sure I wanted to—a slippery thought was bestirring in my mind. A relationship is more than just Andy plus Ann. It is its own self. And in considering what this entity needed, I might have to give up what I wanted. That was my fear. My Pushmi-pullyu would need mountain air and I would not be able to go to the beach.

That night Andy and I went out to dinner. In between sips of wine and furtive glances across the table, I was uncomfortably musing about "relationship," our relationship, the one that seemed very difficult to see in the warm cozy gloom of the candlelit restaurant. I knew I could no longer avoid turning up the lights and looking over there at the other half of it, at him. Really look at him. Worse than that, I would also have to look at myself. And I might not like what I saw, especially over there. What then? Changing houses or husbands did not appear to be the answer. I had already done both.

Driving home, I thought about where I was living (and still am), and how I had placed myself in a community of forty-eight people, placed myself into a room of mirrors, forty-eight mirrors to be exact. I had only to look in them and I could gather as much useful information about myself and my closest relationship as I could stomach. "Might as well look," I said to myself on the way to our house.

I do not think I could have found a better place to begin looking. Since one can only see a relationship against a backdrop of "group," and only see oneself against the backdrop of one's relationships (of which I had a variety here), I had at hand what was needed. Besides, for the first year and a half, we lived in a house consisting of one 10' by 12' room and a small doorless bathroom to which I had added a tiny frig and a hot plate on a table. While Andy took a bath in a tub with four feet, I cooked dinner beside him. It was intimate. On the rainy evening of our second argument, all I could do was to stalk into the bathroom. There was not even a door to slam! Right then it became obvious that if this bright new close relationship were to survive, not to mention grow and flourish, I had a lot of looking to do.

Because our community has so enriched my interior landscape and therefore this book, I will say something about it. In the spring of 1968, a group of people, most of them artists, bought an old dude ranch called Rancho Linda Vista. They then began converting the twenty-one run-down, red-roofed adobe buildings into studios and homes. The first time I visited the ranch, I helped shovel what I called manure and the others called horseshit, out of the barn, The next time I learned to run the cement mixer while Andy, two sculptors, and a potter poured a floor.

Converting also included fashioning these individual adults, their children, and an assortment of animals called pets into a community. Like earlier settlers, they quickly learned that in order to accomplish the physical work necessary for them to stay, they had to develop their ability to cooperate. And this had to occur in the face of their preoccupation with the 2-headed, 4-legged creatures with which they had arrived and which were, for the most part, doing poorly. Occasionally who-isn't-talking-to-whom took up so much time the children barely were fed.

Before moving to the ranch, my notion of the perfect community was the fairy Irish Village. You know the place. It is where Happy Folk whistle while they work, and every weed of discord is fastidiously jerked out of the ground without disrupting the tranquil flow for an instant. Their meetings, unlike ours, would sound like pigeons gurgling.

Once on the ranch, I found out a "sense of community" was not brought about by sitting in a circle and thinking loving thoughts as I imagined my Irish villagers did. I still watch it being forged every day out of our readiness to relate to each other directly, face to face, whenever the need arises…in the middle of the one winding road which connects our houses, in the barnyard, at the pool, around a kitchen table. So we keep on weaving ourselves and our relationships into a fabric called community where each thread is clearly visible and contributes to the entire fabric. Having grown up in a family where anger was supressed, I was particularly surprised to learn that a sense of community comes when all the different ways we relate to each other are included, even the weeds of discord.

A few weeks after our candlelit dinner, on a cold Tuesday morning, I was walking back along the path from the mailbox with a letter from a woman's magazine. My second book had just been published and an editor from that magazine was asking me to write an article for them, subject unspecified. Huddled in my coat, I shuffled slowly along, head bent, wondering what I could write about. Rounding a large rock, I saw a ground squirrel sunning himself before his hole. He was stretched out on his belly in the soft dry dirt, his eyes were half-closed, and a few partially eaten mesquite beans were scattered nearby. He looked thoroughly at home. For an instant his skin was my skin. I uncurled in the warmth and safety of his doorway and the cold lay beyond like a discarded garment. Then I noticed his tail was twitching. A few moments went by, each of us stone-still except for his tail. Then he decided he had immediate business elsewhere, turned, and whisked down his hole. Suddenly, I knew what I would write about.

"What I shall write about is 'home'," I said to myself as I continued along the path. "The problem is—where is it? Is it the ranch and the little house where I now live…Or where I used to live and my sons return to visit?" I envied the ground squirrel who had looked so at home in front of his hole. He knew just where to run to. Scrambling up the hill, I realized that this question had been tugging at me most of my life. Yet I did not suspect that looking for home was, in a sense, looking for myself, or that the quest would provide me with primary information about me and relationship.

That afternoon, I was digging in my garden readying it for spring. Memories began to surface…

> I am on a balcony edged with clumps of red geraniums. Across the lake, high mountain peaks glisten against a sky too bright to look at without squinting. I lean on the railing. Below on the terrace, my school roommate is drinking tea with her father. I wish I had on her ruffly pink dress embroidered with roses. My mother steps out of her room and says, "Dear, yesterday Uncle John cabled that our house has been sold." I burst into tears.

I was eight and my world had just collapsed. Up to that moment I had not minded my mother being a wandering woman. I had not minded growing up in two languages, nor living in many places, because home was always "back there." It was the big white house with thick walls planted firmly in the ground and where a friendly Santa Claus came down the chimney, in English.

Next I recollected a long Thanksgiving table. I had been invited to dinner and to spend the day.

Squeezed in between an old man and a tall pimply boy, I have trouble cutting my turkey. They talk over my head about cars. Then everyone starts planning a picnic which is to take place the very next day—after I am gone! I hardly taste the fresh berry pie. Instead, I sorrowfully contemplate myself as the homeless orphan in my old story book. Wrapped in a ragged shawl, I too stand barefoot in the snow with my nose pressed against a window-pane while inside merry children play Blindman's Buff.

This developed into my favorite posture. It had a refrain attached to it: "I don't care; I don't need anybody!" This did not lead me easily into close relationships. What I wanted to be when I grew up was a gypsy. I would live in a brightly painted gypsy van pulled by a big white horse and as I drove along, children would wave and envy me. I would never be lonely.

The memory that followed was of a small seaside hotel. I was sitting on the front steps beside a plump, bright-eyed girl of six who had been living in the hotel with her parents for a year.

"Here you hold Fritz," the little girl says, handing me a doll in a white sailor suit. "Maria," I say to her, taking the doll and putting it on my knee, "Don't you mind not having a home?" "Oh, but I do have a home," Maria answers, gazing at her parents walking arm in arm nearby in the garden. "Only I don't have a house to put it in." She jumps up, hold out her arms, and I give Fritz back to her. She runs to join her parents. I watch them welcome her. Together they walk off through the hollyhocks. I decide to go for a swim and, kicking stones down the dirt road to the beach, I brood about how at eighteen I don't feel at home with my family. "Well that kind of stuff is alright for Maria. She's just a kid…But I'm not at home with my friends either. Even with my best boy friend I feel a bit off-balance, as if I'm tilting towards him in an effort to please…When I marry and have a house of my own, then I'll be at home!" and I splash into the sea.

At that time I was clinging to my orphan girl role, still tightly wrapped in my shawl of independence which was just beginning to wear thin. To be really close to another was a tantalizing and bewildering notion, but it meant giving up that shawl. Whatever would happen to me then? The next memories surfaced rapidly, one after the other.

I am ambling along a path in hot sunlight and occasionally glancing at my family ahead of me…at my husband who carries the picnic basket and is followed by the dog sniffing the basket…at Peter chatting to his king snake coiled around an arm…at John and Hugh each with a small wooden sailboat…at Michael just in front of me (he is pulling a wagon in which a stuffed rabbit bounces)…at Diana the bobcat who is stalking the bouncing stuffed rabbit. Then my eyes are suddenly jerked to a real rabbit skittering off through the bushes—to his burrow, no doubt. He must have seen the bobcat. Like that rabbit, I now also have a place to run to when cold or afraid. It is my turn to sit at a crowded table and plan a picnic after a visitor has gone.

I kneel on a sidewalk showing my youngest son how to tie his shoes. An old Spanish woman, seated in her doorway, stops knitting to watch us. "Don't do that," she finally says. "If you do, you will set him free and you will be left with your loneliness." Then she goes on knitting.

Walking on a beach towards a full moon, I turn and catch sight of my shadow lying behind me on the sand. I am amazed, and angry, at how clear and sharply defined it is when I feel so mushy and indistinct. I run to a big pine tree. In its shadow I lose my own. Like the woman in a Bushman story who vanished when there no longer was any use for her, I too have disappeared.

Crouched before an open drawer, I do not know what I am looking for. I shut the drawer before remembering.

For a while I reflected on how my carefully spun cocoon of maternity had been dissolving as my sons moved off into their own lives. And there I stood like a ninny wondering what shape to become. I had grown used to my days being formed by household tasks which came ready-made along with husband and children. When those tasks dwindled and my hands lay idle, my days lost their shape, and so did I. Staring into that open drawer, I had decided I was missing something which I needed to find before I could really be at home.

It was as if I had this beautiful necklace and one day I felt a space between the last bead and the clasp. Thereafter my fingers restlessly fiddled with the last bead on the string, moving it back and forth across the gap. Finally I went looking for the bead which I assumed was

missing. You cannot imagine how many I found. But each time I strung my most recent acquisition and put my necklace back on, the gap was there, under my fingers.

I looked in the usual places, in books, brooks, at the feet of teachers—a fancy way of saying I dyed my hair, refurbished the house, attended university classes, volunteered at a hospital, joined a discussion group, wrote a book, had a secret affair, took trips. I remembered how earnestly I looked, and how afraid I had been to touch what my life was brushing against. I had pulled away from my skin and curled up inside. My eyes peeked out gingerly. But here and there I stumbled on an insight. Like a bead, I would string it on my growing rosary of realizations.

I am resting on a fallen Roman column. Next to me a headless woman in marble stands propped against the same column with a ring of blood red poppies around her feet. I reach out and touch her shoulder, feeling the smooth cool curve of it…thinking of the man's hands which had shaped her…recalling a poem:* 'Her hair held earth, her eyes were dark, a double-flute made her move.' I too have been shaped, and today I feel as motionless as the stone woman beside me. Not only have I lost my tasks, I whine, but no one is playing a double-flute to make me move.

In the dark, in the hot moist smelly dark, people are dancing around me. I hate the loud insistent drums pulling on me; I hold my hands tightly over my ears. How can I feel so alone in the middle of so many people? The floor is shaking under my feet. My shirt is wet. What are those tiny bits of light streaking every which way across the ceiling? I wish they'd stop. I wish the drums would stop, and the flailing arms and legs. Why am I here? Who is that screaming?

Two hours have passed since I swallowed the tab of acid and I no longer feel as if I have been grabbed by the back of the neck and shaken. I am watching nine buzzards wheeling slowly around and around directly above. They tilt slightly and turn their heads from side to side, watching me. I can see their beady eyes. My body is heavier than the rock on which I lie, pinned there by the hot round sun. I feel my skin shrivel and gradually fall away, and then the gentlest tickle of ants crawling along my clean bones. Who is that laughing?

*By Robert Creeley

Beside a campfire in a vast and rimless desert, I sit cross-legged watching a nomad woman stir a pot. She has tattoos on her face and a gold ring in her nose, and she can squat comfortably on her heels for hours. I am wondering what would appear before her eyes if I were able to ask her about her home…Would she see herself stirring the pot? Or those with whom she shares the long black tent? Or each piece of desert she nightly borrows and whose silence she fills with housekeeping noises? Or would she see the shifting constellations overhead which her eyes must move amongst as easily as I move amongst the furniture of my house? Suddenly she looks up at me and touches the ring in her nose which glints in the firelight as the rings in my ears also glint, and smiles. Our eyes meet. Looking into their darkness, I feel joined with her and, surprisingly, brought back to myself. How far away I have strayed.

Those remembrances, each one drifting brightly across my eyes, trailed an unexpected assortment of feelings. They formed the building stones of my article entitled *Home, Where Is It?* Near the end, I quoted something Jung once wrote about a woman in Africa. The question did not seem to be where her husband was, but "whether or not she was present in her wholeness." I could not rationally understand that statement, yet his words struck a chord which evoked the presence of the nomad woman. Like the African, she also filled her skin fully, right out to its edges, so that she completely touched whatever was around her. Though she was Arab and her husband owned her, she belonged to herself.

How correctly the word, "belong" expresses it. From 'be' meaning thoroughly, and 'longen' to suit. When one is thoroughly suited to oneself, nothing need be added or erased. And wherever one is, one is always at home. No small thing that, for then we are living in the house of love. We step out from love and do not have to look for it elsewhere. In French, 'at home' is *'chez moi'* …at/with/in me.

The day after I dropped my article in the mailbox, a friend opened our door, calling out, "Are you at home, Ann?" I looked at myself standing in the kitchen with a frying pan in one hand and a spatula in the other, and asked myself, "Am I at home? Am I at/with/in me?...Yes I am, and I forget. I need to be reminded," as an Arab woman had reminded me one night by the firelight, as the hash-brown potatoes just starting to burn reminded me. I laughed somewhat wryly. The degree to which I am at home is the degree to which I am available for the relationship.

Having decided to observe my relationship with Andy, I bought a new notebook with a shiny canary-yellow cover. Next, I looked up the word "relationship." Its Latin root means to 'carry back.' I thought again of the nomad woman and how my intense awareness of her, instead of taking me away from myself, had paradoxically carried me back to myself.

After a few weeks of jotting down some of the things I was noticing about me and Andy, I discovered something else. I was interested! In fact, the more I watched the Pushmi-pullyu to which I belonged the more interested I became. I had my own private Soap Opera unfolding before my very eyes. Month by month my notebook grew fatter.

Shortly after beginning my second yellow notebook, I received a wedding invitation accompanied by a letter from the bride-to-be:

> Living in Rome, I'm going to miss our long conversations on relationship. Somebody just gave me a small book of Household Hints. Now what I need is a book on relationship. *How about it?* I was going to say 'On Marriage', but then I'm also acquiring two step-children, a mother-in-law, and a new boss...It sure has taken me a long time to admit that if I cannot get the basic unit of 1 + 1 to function, everything else in my life functions with difficulty. The simple truth is, when my close relationships are nourishing, my life is a joy.

What Carrie said is true for me too...and that joy ripples out, quickening whatever it touches, like a warm spring wind in my garden.

Indeed, the whole world, everything around us, is experienced and expressed in relationship. It actually takes relationship for me to express myself (which I do when I touch Marmalade, the cat), and to experience myself (which I have done when I am aware of my hand as well as aware of the cat). Yesterday I was outside under a newly leafed mulberry tree scraping paint off a chair. Andy sat nearby repairing his electric saw. And all around us tiny leaf shadows flickered. I turned to say something about this to him. Our eyes met...then we were smiling together. The sunlight was warm on my back. For that moment, nothing was missing.

Coincidental to the arrival of Carrie's letter, Andy and I had been uncovering some basic truths or aspects about the nature of our relationship. We were noticing that our awareness of these enhanced our life together. So we had them inscribed in calligraphy and sent them to Carrie as part of her wedding present.

For weeks afterwards, Carrie's "How about it?" rattled around in my head. Then I received a letter from a doctor friend who works for Unesco in the area of world health. He wrote bemoaning the amount of time and energy spent, in his office, handling who-isn't-talking-to-whom. "So you want to know how to make the world work?" he concluded, "Have your relationships work...by which I mean, be satisfying. Sometimes I think that's where the real hunger lies." He had just provided a context for a book that Carrie had suggested I write.

Contrary to my first book, which was written mainly for my sons, and the second which was written mainly for myself, this one is written for you and me, in the light of the mind's sorting. What follows is a personal journey, or more accurately a stroll, a leisurely ramble through the landscape of relationship. Everyone of us is wandering around in that landscape with our Pushmi-pullyus in tow. Though mine may at first appear to be strange to you, still, the elements of which everything is made will be familiar.

For a compass I will be using questions: What does enhance a relationship's quality? To what am I committed? Which are the questions that open doors to new possibilities? In the moment of truth before journeys begin, I must tell you that I am travelling with an eye to how my relationships function rather than trying to solve them as if they were a problem. All that this journey requires is our innate ability to observe—as Eric, my grandson who is three, hunkers down and looks at his dog chewing a bone. He just looks.

I will begin with the seven aspects of relationship which we sent to Carrie.

A relationship, like the wind,
has no form.

One 'sees' the wind by watching trees moving; trees
moving are no more the wind than, say, marriage is the
relationship.

A relationship has a tendency to disintegrate.

Like everything else in the universe, a relationship is entropic—meaning it tends to fall apart, to run down.

*A relationship is expanded
by a purpose larger
than its own continuance.*

If your intention is simply its perpetuation, it will indeed
survive, but it will gradually pall. A relationship, to grow,
cannot be about the relationship; it has to have a task or
endeavor in which to express itself. Then it enriches all
that it touches, including itself.

A relationship, like life,
is neither fair nor unfair.

We usually conclude it is not fair since, as everyone
knows, we rarely feel properly thanked or appreciated,
and it hardly ever seems equal.

A relationship is a privilege.

It provides a place, or more precisely a space, in which to express and experience love.

A relationship is a windowpane.

You can see through the window to what is outside and at
the same time, in its glass, see yourself reflected.

*A relationship can ever be
more finely tuned.*

"You and me…together like a fiddle-bow
drawing one voice from two strings it glides along…
O sweetest song.

(from *Love Song* by Rilke)

2. Portraits

Andy came storming out of the bathroom. "Where is my brown jacket?"

"Why I think it's in the closet," I answered.

"In the closet!" he shouted. "I left it on the bathroom chair."

"Yes I know; I found it there. And I hung it up for you," I explained, my voice ever so slightly tinged with self-righteousness.

"You hung it up for me!" he shouted even louder, marching right up to me. His eyes were very blue and bulging slightly.

"Well…well, I…I thought it belonged…" and my voice trailed off as I backed away. That was the beginning of our first fight, six-and-a-half days after we had walked into our first house.

My image of a good wife was one who kept things clean and tidy. After all, that is what my mother did. Andy's image of a good wife was one who left his things alone. He thought that rearranging his things was rearranging him, as if he were not all right somehow.

My image of a good husband was one who did not shout; besides everyone knows that fighting means your relationship is in trouble. Andy's image of a good husband was one who expressed his feelings.

Years later I discovered that though a relationship has no form, even so we fashion pictures out of what our eyes and ears pick up about relationship as we grow up. Example: If I marry Prince Charming, I'll live happily ever after; if I'm not happy, obviously I did not marry my true prince so I had better keep on looking. We lay those pictures on top of our relationships, expecting our relationships to match our pictures. Here barely one week had passed and already my precious tableaus were being overthrown. How upsetting!

I am not suggesting that we get rid of these pictures even were that possible. Personally, I have taken a fancy to mine. I keep them in a special section of my shiny yellow notebook. Every so often I leaf through them and am quite entertained; they are useful. Sometimes I notice I am tugging and squeezing on my family and friends in an obstinate effort to fit them into one of my pictures. (I remember a fairy tale in which young men were captured by an ogre, placed on a bed, and made to fit—either by being chopped off or stretched.) If I confide to my hapless victims what I have been trying to do to them, what would have turned into unpleasant encounters, may instead turn into delightful ones.

I call these tableaus *Portraits of Relationship* and I have asked my ranch family to contribute to my collection. Here are some samples of their pictures as well as mine. The first is my old English portrait. It is a dressed up version of one of the ways I see my relationship with Andy, namely: He as teacher and I as student.

> *Scene I.* She stands in a doorway waving goodby to Him. He is riding off on his horse, her silken handkerchief tied to his left arm and He is carrying a bag lunch.
> *Scene II.* Every day She cooks, scrubs and sweeps. But every so often She leans on her broom and thinks of Him. Every day He rides up and down mountains, crosses rivers, fights dragons, and drinks flagons of grog with his buddies. Every so often He thinks of Her.
> *Scene III.* She is sitting under a blossoming rowan tree and staring down at the dragon's hoard He has just poured into her lap. He stands before Her, an empty sack in one hand and his horse's reins in the other. A dead dragon is draped over the horse's rump.

During a ranch potluck, Peter Read succinctly told me how he saw relationship.

> Two people are riding side by side in a forest. Periodically one of them takes a short jaunt through the trees and rejoins the other further along. They are always in the forest.

At the potluck, Elli, who had been listening, added her portrait when Peter was finished.

> Two friends are tending a garden. It takes a certain amount of attention, but not too much, and care must be taken not to over-water or over-fertilize or the plants will die. Others walk by and say to them, "Oh, you've got weeds in your garden!" They answer, "What you think are weeds are really very good to eat—full of vitamins and minerals."

Here are two portraits from Pat who lives near the windmill. The first she gave to me before she was married, the second a couple of months afterwards.

> *Before.* The drab grey lady bird stays home cleaning and fixing up the nest. The male bird, in bright colors, goes out into the world on exciting adventures and grows ever more brightly colored. When he's tired he comes back to the nest and is recharged by sucking the juices out of the poor grey bird. She eventually dies.
>
> *After.* In a grove of trees and pussywillows, two children are building a fort up in one of the trees. Sometimes they work together, sometimes alone. And sometimes one of them goes and gets more stuff to build with. Neither of them is grey.

A few days ago Pat's husband, Charles, came by with his portrait.

> My portrait of a relationship is pen pals, once removed. One lives in China and speaks no English; the other lives in Arizona and speaks no Chinese. They each write to a third party in Russia who speaks both languages.

I found the following on my kitchen table. It was left by Gerry who wrote at the top of the page, "This is a portrait of me and my friend Emma when we were twelve."

> On the slowly revolving circle of a double merry-go-round, my friend Emma lounges languidly on an ornate swan throne fanning herself. The outer circle zooms around at a breathless speed where I, dressed in a tight leather suit to cut down wind resistance, urge on my charging black stallion. Each time we pass we exchange gold rings. You'd think she'd be too slow to make the split-second exchange. Or I'd be too fast. But we never miss.

When Ann Wiseman was visiting she gave me her eighty-seven-year-old mother's description of marriage.

A fried egg with a strip of bacon across the top.

Nan lives in a tiny house that once was a chicken coop. Here is her portrait of her relationship with her mother.

It is as if my mother and I each live in a windowed sphere spinning around the same sun. Every so often a window of her sphere lines up with a window of mine so that for a brief moment she and I can see each other.

Another ranch friend, who asked to remain anonymous, said of his portrait, "This is the way I wish it were."

She can do everything he can do *almost* as well as he. They build a house together. They build basements and sub-basements, turrets, towers and guest rooms. The house is never finished. They work side by side. Neither of them can hole up alone; the other must be allowed in.

This is the way *I* wish it were.

Scene I. Inside a rose-covered cottage for two, she is arranging flowers in a blue vase and happily singing to herself. Every so often she glances out the window to where he is neatly hung up on the clothesline, and smiles.
Scene II. He and she are sitting at a small table spread with savory dishes, their knees are touching and they are talking animatedly together.
Scene III. Inside, she is arranging flowers in a blue vase and happily singing to herself. Every so often she glances out the window to where he is neatly hung up on the clothesline, and smiles.

For several years Charlotte produced a ranch newspaper called *The Pidgin*. Here is her portrait of the perfect lover.

He covers me with roses. He has picked off each thorn.

A few months before her first child was born, my daughter-in-law Bonnie spent a week on the ranch. She smiled when I asked her for hers. "Let me see…Hmmm, I'm remembering a dream I once had."

My brother and I are playing tug-of-war. We each have hold of a thick brown rope and we are pulling and pulling on the rope. I am hot, sweaty and mad. My hair is in my eyes and I can't see. And I can't let go of the rope to brush it away. First he drags me forward and then I pull harder and drag him forward. It goes on like this, back and forth, for a long time. Suddenly my hands slip and we both fall down. We look at each other in surprise and we realize we are both on the same side and have been for some time.

Ruby Lee's portrait. Ruby Lee is an art collaborative by Pat and Charles. These portraits made their first public appearance in a performance on the ranch in 1980.

A notices B

B is interested, but ignores A

A seduces B

B develops expectations of A

A withdraws

B gets upset with A

A gets upset with B's upset

A notices C

A notices B

B seduces A

A pursues B

B withholds from A

A feels rejected by B

B is perplexed

A seduces C

A and B become "friends"

B wins A back from C

B breaks up with A

A wants B

B wants C

C wants D

D wants E

E wants F

F wants G

G wants H

H wants I

I wants J

J wants K

K wants L

L wants M

M wants N

N wants O

O wants P

P wants Q

Q wants R

R wants S

S wants T

T wants U

U wants V

V wants W

W wants X

X wants Y

Y wants Z

Z wants A

More portraits are to be found in Appendix 1.

3. A Portrait Upset

On a cool September evening Andy walked into the kitchen and stood companionably beside me while I arranged fresh poached salmon and broccoli covered with thick yellow Hollandaise on our dinner plates. I had been thinking about my dream rose-covered cottage for two—for two and maybe one cat. However, we were now living in a large U-shaped house with two dogs and one scraggly rosebush next to the front door. Even so, I was enjoying myself.

I smiled at Andy, put the plates on the table and stood for a moment admiring our new white place mats. "Very pretty."

"What's pretty?"

"The place mats. I like the embroidery."

Andy lit the candles, sat down, cleared his throat and said, "I've just been talking to Jean. Next week my kids are moving in with us."

My heart stopped.

I almost knocked over the candles as I sat down. I thought, "Oh no! Four kids in this house? I just raised four kids!" Silently I spread my napkin on my lap, picked up my fork, and laid it down again. Silently I looked around my nice neat kitchen, thinking of gallons of milk and sticky jars of peanut butter crowding my nice neat frig. Through the open door I could see a copper bowl full of chrysanthemums and bright pillows invitingly plumped on the couch in my nice neat quiet living-room that suddenly seemed to fill with coats, sneakers, half-done homework, the blare of TV, doors slamming…Then I went numb. I felt cold, clammy and dizzy; I wanted to bolt. But then Andy lived in this house. "Oh that's nice," I finally managed to squeak out. "Do have some biscuits." I had retreated inside myself and politely shut the door.

The following week Maggie, Joe, Sam and Ben, ages nine to fourteen, moved in. Some very painful months crawled by. No matter how polite I was, how warmly I smiled, how well I cooked and did my duty, as long as my inner door was shut, it all turned sour. Yet my whole body shuddered at the thought of opening that door, of letting Andy's kids be close to me. Of course I could leave and find another man. But I could be sure something would happen and I would again be behind my door. Stuck, that is how I felt, like a bug on a pin. Ultimately there was nowhere to go.

Gradually my door creaked open.

It was spring. We—Andy and I—were sitting under an oak enjoying the warm silky air and the flowers. I was inviting him on a camping trip to Libertad—to lie on a beach, swim in a sea, gaze at boojum trees and porpoises. I would plan it, provision it, and execute it, I assured him. He was to be a pampered guest..."And maybe help just a tiny bit with the firewood?" I asked slyly. (Camping is my passion and I consider myself adept at it.) Then, to my surprise and horror, I added, "Let's invite the kids to go with us."

So I did, and they went. All six of us gazed at boojums and watched porpoises leaping out of the sea. Joe and I built a sandcastle with seven turrets and a drawbridge. Sam took me to see an osprey nest. Maggie made me a shell necklace. Ben, the silent one, lit the breakfast fires. We all skipped rope with long slimy lengths of seaweed. And at night, by the firelight, I read aloud of hobbits, with the younger kids nestled beside me like small furry animals.

A few weeks afterwards, we were invited out to dinner. "Oh I'm sorry, but we promised our kids we would all go to the movies," I answered, glancing at Andy for confirmation. He had a funny expression on his face; I thought I had made a mistake. "That's right, we did promise," he corroborated. "It's just that you said 'our' kids."

Soon other children on the ranch were moving in and out of our lives, and their parents, and Andy's students, and an ever widening circle of friends—each one tilting my portraits and also adding something special. My relationship with Andy quickened when I shared it, when I welcomed others into it as I might welcome a guest into our house. I laughed outloud the day I noticed buds on the scraggly rosebush by the front door. The next morning it was sprinkled with scarlet blossoms.

Looking back on the years that Andy's children lived with us, I realize how much easier it was to raise stepchildren, once I had opened my inner door and let them in. It was easier to make room for them to be exactly as they were. I remember the first time one of them, I think it was Sam, went to school dressed in a style of which I disapproved. To my surprise, I was not upset. "Odd," I said to myself, "Had that been John I would have fussed until he changed his shirt and the air would have been stormy for hours." In those days I presumed my concern came out of my love for my sons. Now I can see that love is not at all like that. My concern rose out of my fear that if John went to school in such a shirt, people would think less of me. Just the other morning I watched a woman carrying a screaming child out of a store. Her eye caught mine and she blushed.

I remember the afternoon Joe came into my studio very upset and crying. I actually let him tell me what had happened without trying to reason him out of it, or trying to put a bandaid on his heart. I was so emotionally entangled with my own sons that I rarely made room for them to go through such painful things as anger and disappointment. Though this has not affected the love we have for each other, it has affected the quality of our relationship. There is a restraint, a carefulness, not present in my relationship with Andy's children.

A few days ago I went for a walk with Eric, my three-year-old grandson. He ran down the path, tripped on a stone and fell. Terrible heart-rending howls. With great effort, I kept myself from swooping him up and kissing his bumped head, "to make the hurt go away." Instead, I sat down close beside him. After a bit he crawled into my lap, still crying. Soon the crying subsided into sniffles and periodic squeaks. Then silence. We sat for a few minutes in the warmth of the sun. A cactus wren in a nearby bush began to scold. Eric lifted his head, rubbed it briefly, got out of my lap, stood up, smiled, pulled at my hand, and we were off again on our walk.

4. Upsets

"By the way," Andy said early one Saturday afternoon as he helped me carry the groceries into our house. "The Watsons called while you were shopping. They want us to go out to dinner with them before they leave for New York."

"Wonderful, I'd love it. Maybe we could try that new restaurant on Miracle Mile."

"The trouble is I have a Hunger Project meeting on the only night they can go."

The resulting argument ended when he said, "No reason why you can't go." We parted in a huff, he to his studio and I to my desk. As I passed the bookshelves, my eyes fell on pink paper lying beside the dictionary "Oh...there are the questions Louisa sent me...weeks ago...and I haven't thanked her." Nor had I read beyond the large block letters she had printed on the first page: THINGS TO ASK YOURSELF WHEN YOU'RE REALLY MAD AT SOMEONE. "Well I sure am mad at him right now," I grumped to myself. "But who wants to answer questions at a time like this. What I want to do is cut him up in small pieces and flush him down the toilet." (A relationship tends to disintegrate.)

For the rest of the afternoon my thoughts hung in the air like smoke. "He's out there saving the world and our house is burning down." I stirred the stew bubbling on the stove. "No time for me, eh! That worm...I'll show him...I don't care. Who needs him anyway." I made an apricot pie with toasted almonds on top. Later, I placed the pie before him, smiling, and inside I hardened my heart.

31

After dinner, Andy offered to wash the dishes. I cleared the table, wiped it, spread out a length of pale green silk on which I had pinned a pattern, and proceeded to cut a blouse. Andy came over and placed a bowl of grapes on a stool near to where I was working. "Thanks," I said, keeping my head bent.

"Nice color, that green…matches the grapes." He put his hand lightly on my shoulder. "Are you still upset about my not going to dinner with you and the Watsons?"

"Upset? Not at all." I turned the fabric and cut around a curve. He stood for a moment watching me.

"I think you're mad at me."

"Nope. Everything's just fine." I went on cutting the shimmering silk and the air around us thickened with unsaid things.

Two weeks passed. I was on my way home after a day spent with my second son and his wife Bonnie at their ranch. We had been invited to lunch and Andy was to have ridden their new horse, only he was in Phoenix for the gallery opening of a friend's show. Now it was late afternoon and the sun hung low behind me. My car and I were chasing our lengthening shadow, watched by the single yellow eye of an occasional tall white poppy swaying in the wind of our passing. The light had turned peach.

Usually I savor the day's slide into dusk, but on this Sunday I was thinking about Andy's return from Phoenix the next morning, and how polite, nice and cool I would be. I saw myself in my lavender dress listening attentively to his every word. But he would know something was amiss without being able to quite put his finger on it.

In a corner of my mind, I knew that he could not possibly mollify me, even were he to take me to dinner at Cybelle's, or bring me flowers, or the pearl earrings which I coveted. It was almost as if I had arranged things expressly so that he would do something I could use against him and thus justify my revenge. What I wanted to do more than anything else was to punish him. I shivered slightly, the car bumped across the cattle-guard, and I was home.

While I was dusting and putting the house in order, I came across the pink pages of questions sent to me by my friend. Absentmindedly I picked them up, thinking to store them in a drawer. But instead, I sat down and read them, including my friend's two post-scripts at the bottom of the third and last page.

P.S. I strongly recommend saying your answers OUTLOUD. When I do this (feeling ridiculous), my answers come to life so I can really hear them. They roll around in my head stirring up other things that have been lying hidden and forgotten.

P.P.S. Be sure to answer each question SPECIFICALLY AND PRECISELY.

I turned back to the questions and noticed that my head felt tight; so did my throat and chest. Ten minutes later I was picking up the telephone and dialing my friend long distance. "Specifically and precisely!" I groaned. "Impossible...It's all a grey blur...a horrible muddle."

"Hey! You've taken the first essential step—that of opening your eyes. You know, if you weren't looking, you wouldn't have seen the grey blur. So just keep on looking at the questions. Something will emerge...you can be sure," and she laughed. I did not like the sound of that at all.

"But I'm upset about so many things...like this weekend, and his forgetting to buy the cat food, and his not going to dinner with our friends because of some damn meeting...."

"That's fine. Just choose one of those to work with. The important thing is to answer the questions precisely. And don't forget to say your answers outloud, so you can actually hear them." She laughed again and hung up. Now I was mad at her and at Andy.

I decided to scrub the kitchen floor. As I was emptying the bucket of soapy water, the phone rang. It was she. "I've been thinking I kind of dumped those questions into your lap. Do you have a few minutes to talk?" I grunted a begrudging "yes" and she went on to tell me about the first time she used the questions after a fight with her teen-age daughter.

"I hated looking at them so much, I took them to the corner café, sat at a booth by a window and ordered beer. Even then I could hardly work my way through them...I remember having to stop every so often to look out the window. Some little kids were stamping around in a mud puddle...I must have gone to the bathroom at least four times." She giggled, and was quiet for a moment. I could hear Country Western in the background. "Are you there?" she asked.

"Yes. I'm listening. Go on."

"I want to encourage you to use them. Believe me, I know how hard it is to be objective...and truthful...when you're mad. Who in their right mind wants to deliberately bump up against certain things in one-self, or the fact that maybe the person over there isn't wrong after all—especially when that other person is a teen-age daughter!" She cleared her throat. "Now…Jane and I can actually listen to each other. The questions do work. I have learned some unexpected things about my-self and where she and I lock horns…such as when I'm assuming mothers know best." Again she paused. "More than anything else," she continued in a husky voice, "I want my relationship with my daughter to be nourishing to us both. When the going gets tough, I remind my-self of this."

So I sat down with the first sheet of pink paper. After a bit I wrote the answers in my notebook.

EXACTLY WHEN DID YOU FIRST BECOME UPSET?
When Andy said he couldn't go out to dinner because he had a meeting.
WHAT ARE YOUR COMPLAINTS AND ACCUSATIONS?
He won't take me out to dinner. His head's so buried in his projects, he doesn't even see me. He doesn't put the ice cubes back in the frig.…
WHAT ARE YOUR FEELINGS?
I feel hurt, resentful and mad!
WHAT ARE YOUR REASONS AND JUSTIFICATIONS FOR YOUR COMPLAINTS, ETC.?
He had four evening meetings in a row and now it's my turn. It just isn't fair.
WHAT ARE YOUR EXPECTATIONS?
He'd be home more. We'd do more things together. He'd tell me he loves me. He'd know what I needed without my having to point it out to him.

Though I had refused to say the answers outloud, my last one in particular had a familiar ring. I leafed back through my notebook to where I had first described my Prince Charming.

He knows exactly what pleases me before I am aware of it myself, and whenever I need him, he is waiting discreetly at my elbow.

Reading this over, I could feel a smile beginning to tug at my mouth. But I was not yet ready to stop being mad at Andy. He should have gone to dinner with our friends and me! That is what a proper husband would have done.

The next night I took the second pink page into the bathroom to read while I soaked in a hot tub. It had only three lines on it:

COMPLETE THE FOLLOWING SENTENCE:
IF ONLY HE/SHE WOULD ―――――――――――――――――――――
THEN I WOULD ――――――――――――――――――――――――

I scrunched way down so that the water reached deliciously up to my chin. After a few minutes, I heard myself filling in the blanks, outloud! In the bathroom, I heard them clearly:

If only he would take me out to dinner more often, then I would know I mattered to him.

Throughout the night those words whined relentlessly in my ears. I was mortified to sound so snivelly. And I could not avoid the implications my answers were provoking. If he took me out to dinner, I mattered, if he did not, I was a trinket to be lightly put aside. As long as he did the important things (hung up his coat, paid attention to me, was on time for meals, never forgot to latch the gate), then our relationship was splendid. But if he did not do what I wanted, things looked pretty dreary. I was getting the impression that my happiness depended on what he did or did not do. Really, it was most upsetting.

The last page was as follows:

> Should he (or she or it) suddenly appear before your eyes, would you feel
>   warm & loving ☐   upset ☐
> If it's the latter, in all likelihood you are holding on to the point of view,
> "It's his fault," which you are reinforcing with your reasons. Every point of
> view has attached to it a benefit and a cost....

My benefit was: Then I don't have to do anything about it (since obviously he's to blame...after all, he's away so much.) And my cost was: Not letting myself enjoy the things that Andy's activities brought into my life; no fun in our relationship. My throat constricted when I wrote this last sentence in my notebook. I felt sad.

Thumbing through my yellow notebook, I seem to be endlessly stewing and fretting and furtively complaining as my assumptions are shaken and upset. Outwardly I pretend everything is just fine, and the unsaid things breed further storms. It seems as if relationship is nothing but an interminable string of petty disturbances: somebody eats the leftover roastbeef I was planning to make into hash; she hangs up the phone on me, right while I'm talking; when I reach for my hammer it's not on its hook; I go into the living room after washing the dinner dishes to find every seat taken and no one thinks to offer me a chair. For all practical purposes the daily content of a relationship is this embarrassingly paltry minutiae which we seldom mention but which continues to fester inside us—the way he chews his food, the way she starts the car....

The more I work with my friend's questions, and scribble in my notebook, the more clearly I see how effectively I have constructed each upset. First I take the facts—what you might have seen had you been watching. To wit: Inside a kitchen a man opens a closet door, reaches up to where a hammer is hanging on a hook, and takes it down. On the handle ANN has been painted in black. He goes out of the house swinging the hammer. Time passes. A woman opens the same closet door, reaches up and sees the empty hook. "Damn! It's gone," she says. She slams the closet door shut and hurries out of the house. That is what happens.

Onto those facts I add:

A judgement or two (Civilized people return what they borrow.)

At least one accusation reinforced with reasonable justifications (He's a self-centered slob. He didn't even ask me…or tell me. Why doesn't he use his own hammer?)

My favorite interpretation (If I really mattered to him, he'd be careful of my things.)

A few conclusions (I never should have left my first husband. Men aren't worth all the trouble anyway.)

To finish it off, I wrap up the above in Righteous Indignation. Is it any wonder that relationships tend to disintegrate? Finally I hide this magnificent creation, brimming with significance, behind my back. It would not do to admit to being upset. Everyone knows that being upset means there is something wrong with you, especially when you are upset about a relationship. Then I secretly plot my revenge. The next time I talk to my mother, I will describe the incident of the missing hammer in such a way that she will commiserate with all that I have to endure.

However, as you can see, each upset is a gold mine richly veined with invaluable information about myself and my relationships, about my unassailable beliefs and opinions, about my behavior and entrenched reactions. Every argument, every fight, further reveals how I have fabricated my point of view, my reality; and no one can have precisely my point of view unless that someone else squeezes behind my eyes to peer out through them.

By seeing exactly how I have put together each and every rumpus, I am inevitably led to the conclusion that it is not Andy who is causing them, nor the fact that my hammer is missing. Somebody else might not have minded the hammer being gone at all. It is I alone who generate my turmoils, because it is I alone who generate my thoughts and feelings. This is No. 1 in my collection of Disagreeable Truths to be found listed in Appendix II.

In a close relationship, how I manage the other's perturbations is as vital to the health of the relationship as how I manage my own. Usually I rush to pour oil on Andy's troubled waters, trying to make him (and myself) feel better, with very poor results. Right now, suffice it to say that my underlying difficulty is in letting him be upset, though I am learning. Yesterday, I actually watched him storm out of the house without lifting a finger, and without hardening my heart.

After receiving my friend's questions, Andy and I assembled others. Their purpose is to aid us in discovering exactly where we are when in the middle of a disturbing situation, just as a sextant aids a navigator in locating the ship's position. Unless one knows precisely where one is, one cannot determine in what direction to steer. Our questions are listed under Appendix III.

Besides sorting out your thoughts and feelings, these questions will point to what mainly is concerning you at the moment, such as being right, or not rocking the boat further. A word of caution: In order for the questions to work and be worthwhile, one must step out to meet them with goodwill, otherwise the words will lie inert on the page. A number of years ago I bought *Teach Yourself Spanish.* After a week of unsatisfactory evenings, I decided the book was without value. The truth was that I did not join in, and would not commit myself to learning Spanish.

Also included in Appendix III are some questions that you and the person with whom you are upset can ask each other. You will know you have addressed yourself to them wholeheartedly when all that is left to say is, "I love you."

The first time Andy and I used the questions I have just mentioned, we dawdled for a while in the place where the only thing left to say is, "I love you." Then, in the manner of such things, we went on to what was next. For Andy it was working on a new plate in his studio. For me it was canning a basket of tomatoes. As I put on my apron, I mentally dusted myself off with a complacent, "Well, we certainly disposed of that upset!"

Eight sunny October days slipped smoothly by. In my cupboard three dozen jars of tomatoes were stacked; and all was well with my world. On the ninth day I was washing the breakfast dishes and said to Andy, who was feeding the cat, "Would you help me fix my sewing machine?"

"I don't have time for that today...maybe tomorrow," he answered. With a friendly wave, he headed for his studio. And there I was, stewing and fretting in the very same pot as on the day, months before, he had said he could not dine with our friends.

I had run headlong into my second Disagreeable Truth: It is never over. The same upsets recur. You know how you always become irritated when, say, the paperboy throws the newspaper into the bushes instead of onto the front steps? However, on this day, my pot did not seem to be bubbling as violently as before. I could actually stick my head above the surface and see the same complaints, the same justifications and feelings, bobbing about like carrots and onions. Suddenly it occurred to me that whenever something happened that I interpreted as my not-mattering, I became upset. I was out of the pot before Andy returned from his studio. Someday I may be out in a blink of an eye, saying to myself, "Oh yes, there's that one again, old number 17."

Last night I heard rain against the windows and this morning when I opened my eyes and glanced outside, the mountains were gone, with the hills that roll up to them. It was solid fog out there. I could see only the bare, thin, black branches of the silk tree I had planted close to the house. The smooth grey fog had been struck by a mallet, sending out a spider web of lines, just as yesterday my being upset had cracked my smooth grey armour. The cat meowed, wanting to be let in. I stretched, breathed deeply, and got up to open the door.

5. Maintenance
[Latin: to hold in the hand]

"If your car stops, first let it rest," was advice I once was given. "Then if it doesn't go, kick it." The purpose of first letting it rest, my advisor went on to explain, was to make it think you were on its side—the implication being that you were not.

Like my friend, I too believed that anything I had to maintain was my adversary. Maintenance meant toil and trouble. It meant having to undo a small bolt in a freezing wind— a small rusted bolt. Whenever I heard the word "maintenance" I hurried in the opposite direction. That maintenance might mean something other than repair had not yet crossed my mind.

One day I watched Michael, my third son, holding the back wheel of his bicycle in his left hand while he carefully cleaned it with his other hand. "Is something wrong with it?" I asked.

"No, I take my bicycle apart regularly and clean it." Come to think of it, his bicycle always looks brand new. If you want something to stick around, you maintain it. Maintenance is the expression of "I want this relationship to continue." It comes out of love.

We forget that we already are familiar with the experience of maintaining something on a regular basis without waiting for it to break down: As Michael cares for his bicycle, most of us care for our teeth, and I have learned to care for my car. Then I will notice the funny smell, the slightly irritating sound. It is easier to replace a fan belt than an engine and far less costly. I found that out the day I drove home after an argument with a friend.

This incident made it plain that maintenance requires one to be sufficiently disentangled from one's problems to lift one's head and look at what we are maintaining. Effective maintenance comes out of a state of attention. This is harder to achieve than it sounds. Not only do I have to be disentangled from my problems, but I also have to accept what I am looking at just as it is. Otherwise I am preoccupied with how I want to be and will fail to see what is needed—as Andy saw this morning.

I was typing and he came and laid his hands on my shoulders. Suddenly I was aware that they were hunched up and the tension had seeped down my back. Under the warmth of his hands, my shoulders relaxed. I felt lighter; the words seemed to slip out more easily. Later, I took care in fixing his lunch, noticing he was tired. Observation has its rewards.

Did you ever skate hand in hand with a friend who would swing you forward, and then, out of the momentum, you would swing your friend forward? And so you went along together, diphthonging over the ice. That is how our relationship was today. Actually, that is how it is always, only most of the time I am too busy stewing and fretting to notice it.

Andy and I have found that maintenance is made much easier by having available, should either of us want it, a time and place in which to talk safely face to face. What essentially makes it safe for us is having an agreement first, not to be interrupted by others, and second, not to interrupt each other. It is where I can tell the truth without fear of reprisal, knowing I will be heard right to the very, very last drop. Communication is at the heart of maintenance, as well as at the heart of relationship.

6. Communication
[Latin: to make known]

Once I was asked if my son Peter and I were communicating. "Oh no," I answered. "He's much too young to talk." I thought communicating was principally about words. Necessity soon forced me to include squawks, pats, punches, pointing accompanied by grunts, mouth squeezed shut, arms flung wide, and even toys left in forbidden places. Or, as in the case with Andy, tools left in the kitchen. Or, as in the case with Marmalade the cat, his sitting silently in front of a closed door. And in the case with me, the bed unmade. (I can always tell exactly where I am with Andy by how I make or do not make the bed). Really, what a bewildering assortment of messages there are. And each and every message produces a result, though it may not always be the result I expect or want.

Last spring my mother spent several weeks with us. During that time I was on the telephone about an hour each day. I had volunteered to contact inactive members of a service organization and interest them in participating again. Some of my conversations were rather long. I could see my mother was irritated. "When I was young we only used the telephone for emergencies," she remarked several times.

One afternoon, as we were having tea, she asked me what it was like to talk on the telephone so much. I thought for a moment. "Remember the other morning when we watched Laurie weaving…and how she sent the shuttle across the warp from one hand to the other?" My mother glanced at my hands which were imitating Laurie's movements, and nodded. I continued, "Well I send a message across the wire, receive one back, over and over. And like Laurie, I also watch the fabric slowly grow before my eyes. In this fabric of relationship which the other person and I are weaving together, I can see the quality of my communicating, as well as the quality of the relationship. I was just thinking…." Reflectively I again imitated Laurie's gestures. "You know, every so often it's almost as if the other person is one of my hands."

My mother was looking out the window. She turned and smiled. "I'll remember Laurie weaving the next time I'm talking with a friend. Maybe I'll feel differently about the telephone."

Sending a message can be like throwing a ball. The trick, if one wants it to be caught, is to have it plop right into the hand of the receiver. Children test your communicating skills admirably. One day I said to my first-born, forming my words clearly, "Peter, don't drop your peas on the floor." But peas were still dropped on the floor. His father said the very same words and the peas remained on the plate. Obviously something was wrong with my message, and it was not in the words.

Another day I tried, "Don't drop your peas on the floor or I'll spank you!" with no better results. My voice kind of wobbled, ever so slightly. I was breathing faster, my hands were clammy, and thoughts skimmed rapidly by. "What if he throws his peas anyway, what then?...Well, it doesn't really matter, I can easily sweep them up...I never did like peas...maybe Peter won't like me if I...." Uncertain and apprehensive, that is what I was feeling. And what I was communicating. I was caught up in uncertainty. The price of being unaware of my total message was an erosion of the quality of my relationship with my son.

Later in life when Andy's children were under our roof, I could say "Don't leave your shoes in the kitchen!" with excellent results and without even raising my voice. My messages were delivered cleanly, without a lot of unrecognized and unexpressed feelings hidden behind them. One always knows if this is so by the results: no shoes in the kitchen.

But sometimes one does not want one's message to be caught. Once I was given a wooden paddle with a small rubber ball attached to it by a long elastic. Every time I hit the ball it snapped back so I could hit it again. Sometimes my words are like that ball; they have long elastics tied to them so they cannot possibly be caught. Therefore, one needs to release the words and let the receiver have them—as I did not do with Babs.

She arrived on the ranch assuring us that she was eager to live here. Then she would not follow rules. I said, "Look Babs, you can't block that path just because you want to." I said, "Look Babs, the rule here is one dog to a family, not two." I said, "Look Babs, you can't build a new room without consulting the rest of us."

Every word I threw at her was tied to a rubber band. It snapped back into my hand so I could hit her with it again and continue to keep her in the wrong. I also made it impossible for her to hear what I was saying because I was covertly communicating to her along with my words, "I don't like you. I wish you'd leave." You know how it is when somebody tells you "Don't throw the peas," and the tone of voice sets your teeth on edge? You will look at that person straight in the eye, if you are like me and like Babs, and you will deliberately drop your peas one by one. Someone else says precisely the same thing and the words slip smoothly into your ears. This person seems on your side; of course you do not drop your peas.

So I am responsible for whether or not I am heard. By not letting Babs hear my words I also prevented her from seeing that her behavior was antagonizing most of the community. Actually I wanted her to keep on antagonizing the community, then I could justify continuing to dislike her. The fabric she and I wove together was murky and jarring. It sent ripples of discord throughout the ranch. Months later, when she left, I felt a quick surge of gratification, but no stick-to-the-ribs satisfaction. I kept looking back over my shoulder and seeing a missed opportunity. To tell the truth, I was sad.

The other side of sending a message is receiving it, which brings me to my word-proof vest. I discovered it the day Andy and I were driving back from visiting his daughter Maggie at school. We stopped for a picnic beside a shallow stream and after eating, we sat for a while on its grassy bank. I was watching the water slipping around rocks and Andy was telling me about this conversation with Maggie concerning her summer plans. Then I interrupted him, "Yes, yes, but don't you see...." And I grabbed what he was saying and galloped off with it in another direction leaving him hanging.

Usually Andy jumps back at me with "There you go again with your 'yes buts'... You're not safe to tell things to!" This time he was silent. Suddenly I heard my voice going on and on. I stopped. I glanced over at Andy.

After some discussion, quite a bit of discussion, we backed up and Andy began what he was telling me again. I started to get restless, to throw pebbles into the water. Important thoughts loomed in my head, so important that if I did not tell them immediately, Andy would be in trouble, and the sky would fall down. I felt very anxious. And there I was, not listening again. With effort I re-opened my ears. But soon what he was saying was outrageous to me, totally wrong! Anger welled up and immediately my ears closed. I would not let in one more word. In fact, his words were ricochetting off me and to my amazement, I saw I had on a word-proof vest.

I realized that was how I always protected myself from hearing what I did not want to hear. My word-proof vest protected my opinions, beliefs and what I wanted. It protected me from feeling certain feelings, uncomfortable feelings.

This time I took off the vest. I actually allowed Andy's words in; I admitted them. Well, most of them. It was as if I were standing on a stone in the middle of the stream and Andy's words were beckoning to me. But to follow I had to step to the next stone; and I did not want to. I was used to where I was. Besides, my stone was the right stone, good and solid. Every time I heard Andy's words and glanced down at the moving water, I felt dizzy. At last unexpectedly, I stepped. A wave of vertigo... and I was safely on a brand new stone. Things looked different from there. I could see a clump of red flowers that had been concealed behind a stump.

Later in the car, Andy spoke of feeling sad. Now that Maggie, the last of his children, was away at school, he had been looking back at places where he thought he had failed them. Tears were in his eyes; my stomach knotted. But standing on my new stone I received what he was telling me and let it slide quietly through me. "Oh that's how it is with him today. It doesn't mean I have to do anything about it, like trying to make him feel better," which is what I usually do with those closest to me. Then a shift occurred, from my receiving something from another person to my listening as if Andy were me speaking (a subtle distinction.) Suddenly we were dancing together—that is how I felt—and the day sparkled around us.

If I want Andy to tell me what he is feeling, I must make it safe enough for him to reveal himself, as a sea anemone opens in a quiet pool. On the other hand, if I want him to hear me, I must also make it safe enough for him to open his ears. The simple fact is that one of the things that determines the quality of a relationship is the degree to which I assume responsibility for communicating—for both my hearing and being heard, however unfair this seems.* The essence of communication is listening; even when we speak we are listening... or attending. I like the word 'attend'. Its root is 'to stretch'. It thus suggests to me the possibility of reaching beyond my boundaries to include another—in the curious alchemy called "being together."

*This is my third Disagreeable Truth. See Appendix II.

The summer I was thirteen, my mother sent me to dancing lessons at Arthur Murray's. My instructor was Italian. He called me Anna. Halfway through my first lesson he stopped and turned off the music. For one terrible instant I thought he was dismissing me. He said, "Not bad. You have possibility," and I went on breathing.

"The difficulty is, Anna, that you resist what is natural to you. You resist listening." He looked down at his feet for a moment and then directly at me. "We must listen to all of it—especially to the Gravity. And yes even to the little currents of air. Dancing is listening, Bambina." I smiled meekly and nodded, "Yes, Mario." But I had no idea what he was talking about. Weeks later when we were waltzing, I felt like thistledown. Stranger yet, I had no sense of who was leading whom. This was bliss. At the end of the waltz, Mario said, "Bravo Bambina! Now you are listening."

Right now you may be recalling a time when you had a similar experience of exhilaration and deep satisfaction. It may also have been while dancing, or while making love, or while walking down a street. It comes naturally to all of us, but we keep forgetting that we can engender it in ourselves anywhere and anytime. We do not need moonlight and roses, though granted, they add a very nice touch.

These days when my back stiffens, my stomach muscles tighten and my breathing grows shallow and rapid, I know that I am resisting listening. I have just put on my word-proof vest; it impedes my dancing.

I have just remembered an evening at our kitchen table when Andy was telling me about a ranch meeting I had missed. A friend from California was present and after my third interruption she said to me, "Ann, you don't have to either agree or disagree. You can just listen."

For a moment I stared at her blankly; then I laughed. "In my family you had to either agree or disagree...to prove you were intelligent and could form opinions."

Yesterday I had agreed to type some letters for Andy. Later, when he asked me to do it, I did not want to. I tightened my mouth, grabbed the rough draft out of his hands, plunked myself down in front of the typewriter, and let out a long sigh. Andy just stood there. I turned around, glared at him, and said quite loudly, "Don't worry. I'll get it done all right!" He nodded.

I said a wee bit louder, "My back hurts. I've been weeding the garden all morning." He nodded.

I said, louder still, "I should never have agreed…especially since I've so much to do." He nodded. I could feel him right there, following along with me.

I said, "Typing business letters is so boring. Besides, you're very fussy." He nodded. I wanted to grab those words back and throw them at him again. But I let him have them.

I said, "You know, I really don't want to. Don't want to!" Then I started to laugh. I remembered reading a few days ago: No one said you had to like it in order to do it.

Every word I threw at him he had absorbed until I had nothing left to throw. The Bible says that he who gives is blessed. I say, he who receives is thrice blessed. When someone takes what I have offered, particularly when it is my mistrust and anger, I feel unlocked from a position I have been frozen in. I can suddenly breathe fully again, move and step out into my life again…in Seven League Boots.

7. An Unfinished Conversation

"Let's go camping next weekend," I suggested to Andy one night.

"Well, I don't know… the truck has to have new tires before we can take it anywhere. And I'm way behind in the studio. Maybe next month…." Then the phone rang, Andy answered, and a half hour later he was still talking. I went to bed.

The next day started out bright and cheery. Birds were singing, butterflies flapping about, flowers nodding in a soft breeze. Andy and I decided to install a new watering system for the garden. He moved a ten-foot board in one direction while I was moving it in another; my fingers got scrunched. My foot stepped on his toes as he was glueing two plastic pipes together. His elbow whacked my head as I was holding a board for him to saw. I did not clean the pipe-ends to suit him; he definitely did not put them together correctly. The quick easy job stretched into miserable hours. At two o'clock we stopped for lunch and decided to finish the job some other time. I slumped through the rest of the day glowering glumly at my feet. Birds, butterflies and nodding flowers had all disappeared. This relationship of mine was not the way I wanted it. Maybe it was time to visit my mother?

"Please pass the salt," Andy said, breaking the silence at dinner that night. I thought to myself, "Hmmmm, he doesn't like the soup."

Outloud I said, "I have a headache... must be from the sun. It was so hot where we were working."

"Why didn't you wear your hat?"

I shrugged. After a while I interrupted the silence. "By the way, last night I wanted to talk about camping, but you were on the phone."

"I wanted to talk about camping too, after I had done phoning, only you had gone to bed... and carefully over on your side I might add."

I pushed my plate away, leaned on the table and glared angrily at him. "The trouble is we never have time to just be together!"

"Why we just spent the whole morning together in the garden, for Christ's sake. And all of last weekend!"

"The last weekend? You mean driving ten hours in a van with six other people? And then sharing one hotel room and every single meal with them? And then sitting through two whole days of meetings with a hundred and twenty-two people whom you know and I don't? That's not my idea of being together!"

"So how do you define 'being together'?"

"Having your undivided attention, that's how!" (Once again I remembered my portrait of Prince Charming who delights in heart-to-heart talks.)

"Well, for me," said Andy, "'being together' includes any time we are engaged in a mutual project, whether or not we are physically close or others are present."

"How about if you're in another room talking to other people?"

"Yep."

"Or miles away?"

"Yep."

"Or on the other side of the world?"

"Yep."

Two different points of view—just as I, standing on my stone, think cats are for catching pack rats, and Andy on his stone thinks cats are for sitting on laps. The trouble was not that we had two different points of view, but that they were concealed and breeding feelings which were also concealed. Our discussion revealed Andy's resentment that I had not thanked him for having included me in a remarkable weekend; and it revealed my actual appreciation of the weekend. Even though it was not my idea of "being together," I had enjoyed myself. During our discussion, my notions of being together had been jostled. I had to admit that sometimes, even after Andy and I had been face-to-face, I felt empty and disgruntled. What was it, anyway, to be together?

Since unfinished conversations tend to throw sand into the gears of a relationship, busy people cannot afford them. The more Andy and I have to do, the more care we need to take, especially regarding resentments. Often I push these aside. "Oh that's too small (or silly) to mention," I say to myself as I rush on to something else. However all my unspoken resentments pile up in a corner of my mind and soon I have a volcanic eruption on my hands.

Thank-yous which are not given or received also put sand into the gears. To my surprise I am finding how often I do not give or receive thanks. "I'll be dammed if I'll thank him for fixing the sink," I muttered to myself a few days ago. "After all, he's supposed to do that... and I had to remind him twice." Last night Andy came into the bedroom where I was reading and said, "Thanks for sewing the button on my shirt."

"That's okay," I answered. This time I heard myself brushing off his thanks. I put down my book, faced him squarely and let his thanks sink in, squirming so visibly that we both laughed. Is it not amazing how difficult this is to do? How difficult it is to let ourselves be thanked and appreciated, as if it were some debt we would have to repay.

When I look, Andy shows his appreciation in many different ways, by stamping and mailing my letters, for instance. Sometimes he pours out that kind of thanks and it is like pouring water down a rat hole. I will turn around and accuse him of not appreciating me. My fourth Disagreeable Truth is that I will never feel fully appreciated until I can appreciate and acknowledge myself. Furthermore, it is up to me to feel appreciated out of the circumstances at hand. I say to myself, "Taking me out to dinner counts, not fixing the sink."

Without a doubt, unexpressed and unreceived thank-yous and resentments leave holes in the fabric of relationship and soon it becomes a rather breezy affair. It would hardly keep a baby rabbit warm.

A few mornings after the button episode (when I brushed off Andy's thanks), I was slouched in my studio chair eating an apple and admiring April's new feathery mesquite leaves. All five of my windows were filled with them; they trembled ever so slightly. Outside the highest window a male quail sat in this pale jade bower calling plaintively to his lady love. The sudden flight of the quail was followed by a knock on my door. I said, "Come in," and Andy stepped inside.

"Sorry to interrupt you... I just wanted to apologize for the way I blew up at you this morning."

"Oh that's okay," I answered, brushing off his apology as I had brushed off his thanks a few nights before.

"May I sit down for a minute?"

"Sure."

He sat on the couch. "Now let me say that again. I apologize for the way I blew up at you this morning."

I looked at him in silence and then nodded. "Thanks for coming to tell me. I forgive you." At that moment I realized I had been barricading myself against him all morning for suddenly the wall crumbled and love rushed in. Andy smiled, got up and went out the door, closing it carefully behind him.

After he left, I continued watching the mesquite leaves. I could not remember ever having said "I forgive you" before. The words scraped on my ears like a fingernail on a blackboard. Only arrogant presumptuous people said such things.

Weeks later I heard someone say that our principal job on earth was to forgive. This rattled around in my head for days. I even made a list in my yellow notebook of people I had not forgiven. It was as simple to do as the litmus test we performed in my high-school science class (blue for bases, red for acids). I would summon up a face and either I felt pleased or a quiver of resentment. Next to some names I wrote down what I was still upset about. Then a thought darted into my mind: what I had not forgiven them for was also what I had not forgiven myself for.

Forgiveness means to give up resentment or the desire to punish. It does not include extracting a promise from the one being forgiven never to do "that" again. Just as the most difficult person to thank and appreciate is oneself, so too the most difficult person to forgive is oneself. For years I would not forgive myself for quitting my first marriage. I contrived this to mean that Andy therefore was not really my husband. The benefit I derived from this conclusion was a justification for the times I wished to shut him out, or for any other unwifely behavior. The cost, once again, was in the quality of our relationship, as if a window had slowly grown cloudy. I do not notice this until the day it is washed and I peer through a clean window to a startlingly sharp, bright world.

8. To Make Oneself Known

Occasionally I stop by Laurie's studio to visit and watch her weave. Along one wall skeins of yarn are piled on shelves, making vivid splashes of color. My eyes run over the blues, greens and purples to the pinks, to the yellows, and then on to the oranges, reds and rich earth browns. Yesterday on her loom a canyon scene was growing. I marvelled at the skillful shift of colors and thought, "Were she afraid to use puce or soot black, the results would be far less satisfying."

A long time ago I stuffed my puce-red anger in a bureau drawer and only let it out in tiny pinches of resentment. Gradually I was able to let my anger pass through me like a wind. I could experience it without holding on to it and enlarging it. I also could express it without wounding those around me. The more I did this, the more I could experience and express my love.

It has taken me years to let certain things out of my bureau drawer. My heart for one. When I was eight I made fun of girls who played with dolls, who giggled and cried and were always hugging. I called that "mushy stuff." Their mothers called me heartless; I believed them. Like the Tin Woodman, I supposed I would have to go to Oz to get a heart, but I did not really want one then. Oddly enough, at the same time I was secretly accusing my mother of having no feelings. Around our house we were not demonstrative.

63

That was pretty much the way things were until after I moved to the ranch. Concurrent with observing my relationship with Andy, inevitably I took heed of my other close relationships, especially the one with my mother. Every spring and fall I visit her in Santa Barbara. During one of these visits, we had a huge argument. I insisted on doing something she did not want me to do. All the way home in the airplane I fretted. This time I did not bury the discord in my bureau drawer.

While I waited for my suitcase I telephoned my mother. I told her how silly I felt, this fifty-year-old woman arguing with her mother as if she were six. I apologized. As I was talking, I had this funny feeling in my chest. I could see, in my mind's eye, my mother… sitting in her chair with one hand in her lap, the other holding the phone…looking at me just a bit anxiously…her mouth curled up at the corners as if about to smile. I could feel how small she was when I hugged her, and how light. Then, for the first time I can remember, I was saying to her, "Mother, I love you." There was this long silence. My mother (whom I used to accuse of having no feelings) then said, "Well dear, I feel very weepy right now…."

I stepped out of the phone booth and a waiting woman said, "My, you look as if you've heard good news."

"Yes I have," I answered. "I've been talking to my mother and discovered at this late age that we each… have a heart. A touchable heart." We laughed somewhat awkwardly together. She entered the phone booth, turned around and said, "I'm calling my father." Her voice shook. I nodded.

All the way home I felt the strong beat of my heart.

This incident brought something else into the light. When my mother said, "You look wonderful, dear, but don't you think you should clean your fingernails," or, "What a lovely dress, but what about your shoes," I heard those words as criticism. I felt anger, which of course I hid. I would then punish her by withdrawing behind cool politeness. After this last visit, it occurred to me that what she was really expressing was her concern for me. What a difference it makes when I hear what she says as another way of her telling me she loves me.

I have been thinking of Babs and my past encounters with her. What I most disliked about her was her obstinate pursuit of what she wanted. She bulldozed her way straight ahead with no regard at all for who or what might be in her way.

"Of course you disliked her; she's just like you," Charles (who lives next to the windmill) said to me after listening to my grumblings. "Now me—I like and admire you both."

It took me until the next afternoon to admit to Charles that what he had said was true. Around Babs I was the one being shoved aside—a very disagreeable sensation. Actually, people are mirrors standing around for us to see ourselves in. Perhaps we should bless the people we condemn because they reveal to us the hidden aspects of ourselves we consider to be unacceptable.

Remember the last time you were at a party and across the room you saw someone who annoyed you? The other evening I saw a woman whom I have long disliked. She had settled herself in an armchair and was hunched forward talking to a girl seated on the floor listening. The girl looked very uncomfortable. I poked Andy who was standing beside me. "Look, there's Carmen gossiping and spreading her poison as usual. She's like a spider…." Andy nodded, smiled blandly and turned to speak to the person on his right. I blushed.

It is as if I have this closet in which every skin in the world is hung—all the different roles to play, from saint, to gossip, to the most depraved killer. In the front are the respectable ones, those I like: devoted wife, faithful friend, wise mother. Way in the back are the ones I am afraid of and despise. They are all there, every single possibility, all waiting to be donned. Were it not so, I would not know compassion, or love.

I think of a Christmas morning that sixteen of us from a service organization spent in the State Prison yard with five hundred men. When the gates clanged shut behind us, I wanted to scurry down a hole. I could see the guards in their towers. Overhead the sun was very bright and all our shadows lay sharp and clean on the hard bare ground. Feeling embarrassed I slowly walked towards a small group off to the left. One of them laughed. Then a tall stately man beckoned to me and smiled. As I approached he moved aside so I could join them. "My name is Frank," he said. Soon we were all talking and even joking together, me and six prisoners who were taking pains to make me feel welcomed. I had come to bring Christmas to them and they were bringing Christmas to me.

When I was serving punch, I noticed Frank standing nearby holding a plate piled high with cake and purple grapes. He was staring upwards. I followed his eyes to a high-flying plane passing silently overhead, and I held my breath waiting for his face to express the longing I expected him to feel. Instead, he exuded such stillness, such tranquility, that for a moment the prison yard seemed quiet. Then our eyes came down together, he looked at me and winked. Maybe he rests in the wide indifferent sky.

9. Help and Support

The morning of our first Christmas Eve party, I was baking cookies. Andy passed by, paused and said, "When you're done, let's take a short walk. We could use a few quiet moments together."

I shot him a quick glance. "Sounds nice, but with the party tonight I've a lot to do." He watched me stir the batter.

"Why don't you get the kids to help," he suggested.

"By the time I tell them what to do, and then make sure they do it right," I answered sourly, "it's easier to do it myself." He shrugged and went out the door. Like the Little Red Hen, I was positive that the only sure way was to do it all by myself. Therefore I spent a lot of time doing things alone while my secret mosquito voice buzzed inside my head. That morning it was saying, "Oh you poor, poor thing. How can he be so insensitive. Of course you can't go walking when you're so busy." Back in a dark corner an even tinier voice (which I ignored) whispered, "How come you're always too busy to spend a few quiet moments with him?"

However Andy's suggestion and the notion of help stayed with me. It had unpleasant implications. Letting myself be helped meant that I was unable to do it, which lessened me in my eyes as well as in the eyes of others. Being helped also meant that then I was indebted to the person who helped me. Whenever I thought about help, I felt as if hooks were being imbedded in my flesh.

Two days after the party Andy said, "You know, you're surrounded with help and support. The trouble is, you just don't admit it."

"What do you mean!" I answered indignantly, for I prided myself on being able to do things all by myself.

"What about the air you breathe, to begin with? And the ground you walk on?"

"But… the air and ground don't count," I sputtered. But the truth had found a crack and slipped in. The next morning on awakening, I noticed how tight my body was—as if, by God, I would never let the bed have my weight. And outside the window, high above the hills, a hawk was resting on the wind.

Whenever I looked outside the window, in the days that followed, I noticed the interconnectedness of things. I could see that nothing stood alone. Everything naturally supported everything else, or it would all have fallen down. One afternoon I said to Andy, "Say, I've been thinking about our Christmas party." We were sitting in the bay window eating a late lunch. Outside, a hawk, probably the very same hawk I had watched a few days earlier, was circling above our heads. His tail feathers were spread and shining red in the sun. "I've been thinking how you saw to it that our friends had wine in their glasses. I want to thank you for this. And also for emptying the ashtrays… I guess that's how you support me. I feel like that hawk up there, resting on the wind." And like that hawk, I could look around and notice things I might not otherwise have seen.

Later I saw Andy adding logs to those by the front door; I noticed my gas tank was full after he had borrowed my car; I saw him wiping crumbs off the kitchen table. I was ironing at the time and I could just glimpse him through the partially opened door. I smiled to myself, feeling warm and cared for. A few minutes later, ironing his shirt, I felt the material under my left hand. How crisp it was where the iron had passed. I was actually enjoying myself… ironing a shirt?

Andy's contributions to the household were contributions to me. By noticing these I was admitting him into my life; I felt a faint tingling, as if dormant muscles had been exercised. I remembered a morning when my governess and I were standing outside my mother's closed door. She had a vase of red roses in her hand. Just before she knocked, she handed me the vase. "*Eh bién,* Annette, you carry the roses." With my eyes carefully watching the vase, I walked across the rug to my mother's bed. Carefully I held it out to her, and as she took the vase, I looked up at her face. Her smile enveloped me like warm firelight. I felt very close to her that day. And big and important. I sat on her bed and finally let her teach me to tie my shoes. It took a while, but under her guidance, I managed. Together we proudly surveyed my tied shoes. When I climbed off her bed, she said, "I'm feeling so much better, I think tomorrow I shall get up. Now, how about bringing me your book and I will read to you."

Right now I am thinking of all the times I would not let my mother help me because I was afraid that if I did, she would have power over me. I would be a mere puppet on her string. Ironically, it was by resisting her that I put my strings in her hands. All she had to do was say one thing and, predictably, I would say or do the opposite. My mother's acceptance of the roses was her gift to me; my letting her teach me to tie my shoes was my gift to her. So together we form moments of joining. I feel very full then, and strong.

Early one morning I was down by my studio digging holes for a bamboo fence. Suddenly Joe, Andy's youngest son, was beside me. "Here Ann, let me do that."

I was about to say, "Oh that's all right Joe, I'm almost done," when I caught sight of his face. "Thank you," I said instead, handing him the shovel. He finished digging the hole and while I held the fence post upright against the level, he wedged rocks around it. Together we set the other two posts, mixed cement and filled the holes. Then Joe hurried to get a broken mirror he had been saving. Carefully he imbedded the pieces at different angles in the wet cement ("To reflect the sunlight and surprise you," he said), and next to them we each made a handprint ("Like signatures," he said). Afterwards, I fixed glasses of lemonade with lots of fresh mint and we sat side by side in the shade of a mesquite drinking and admiring our work.

Last summer I saw him showing his girl friend our handprints. He pointed to his with a hand now grown larger, and then he told her about the day we built the fence. She was a city girl and looked up at him, eyes wide with admiration.

10. To Get Off It

One night I returned from a long day of errands in town. The car was full of groceries and I was looking forward to Andy's help in unloading them, a job I hate. Perhaps afterwards we would have a glass of wine together and chat about the day. Walking into the house, I was greeted by a hungry cat. In the living room the TV was on with the sound turned down; magazines littered the floor; a jacket was draped over one chair and a hat tossed into another. In the kitchen the sink was full of dirty dishes and more dirty dishes were scattered on the counter. An uncooked hamburger, in a puddle of grease, looked up at me from a frying pan. An opened package of cheese was hardening on the chopping block amidst a sprinkling of bread crumbs and a few wilting lettuce leaves, at 99¢ a pound. A loaf of bread lay nearby with a melting stick of butter beside it and a couple of knives smeared with peanut butter. And in the bedroom, Le Monsieur lay asleep on the bed, snoring!

I was outraged. I felt like a pinball machine... all my lights were flashing, all my bells ringing, and T*I*L*T was written across the sky in large neon letters. I stood in the middle of the kitchen with a heavy bag of groceries in each arm trying to find a place to put them. I had to kneel down and put them on the floor. One of the bags broke and spilled in the process. Three cans of soup rolled under a table. By then tears of rage were running down my face and my stomach felt like a knotted rope. "I'll throw up and be sick... I'll get back in the car and go somewhere... I'll clean it all up perfectly and then I'll... I'll sleep in the guest room." Etc. etc. Never had I been so angry. It was as if this man

73

had tramped on the bed-sheets... in muddy boots! That night Andy and I had it out. First I poured out my anger, ending with, "I think you were getting back at me for something." A silence followed. Now it was his turn.

"...worked on an etching for the upcoming show and started a large drawing... Chuck needed help in fixing a broken water-pipe... an unexpected visitor who stayed for lunch... Bozo (a dog) tore a hole in my studio screen-door... getting things out for supper, then thinking I'd have a nice hot bath while the hamburger thawed... feeling very relaxed so stretched out on the bed for a minute. And the next thing I knew, you were, ah... speaking to me."

I listened. Somewhere along, just for a moment, I was in Andy's shoes, and of course the whole thing looked different—even the kitchen! Back in my own shoes, I was beginning to grasp how attached I was to having the house look a certain way, my way, tidy at all times. But now I also had Andy's point of view with me. I still did not like the way the house had looked, only it no longer was a question of who was right and who was wrong. My standard was simply the stone on which I stood, neither right nor wrong. If I want my relationships to grow and flourish, it is always up to me to "get-off-it"—off of the stone where I have to be right.*

Eventually we did have a glass of wine, sitting on the front steps. A great horned owl hooted off to the left, hunting some poor little wood-mouse no doubt.

*See Disagreeable Truth no. 5 in Appendix II.

11. Responsibility
[Latin: to promise in return]

"Poor skinny little thing, she's all knees and elbows," is how my aunt described me to her friends. My mother called me a "feeding problem" and took me to the doctor. Yet as a child I knew perfectly well that it was not the food that made me gag. Somehow, I was making myself gag and I could not stop doing it.

During the second day of the *est* Training, I, Andy, and two-hundred and thirty-three other people were sitting on chairs in a hotel ballroom with our eyes closed. The leader (we called him "the trainer") was taking us on a kind of guided fantasy. Suddenly I was very angry and, in my mind's eye, I saw my mother rocking my baby brother. Her head was bent and she was crooning to him softly. The smell of food cooking permeated the air. I felt like throwing up. Also, I was furious at my brother for being so chubby and huggable, and at my mother for hugging him so much. My fingers itched to pinch him.

By the end of the exercise, it was evident that not only had I made myself gag, I had made myself angry too. After all, my friend Susie, who had a chubby little brother, loved having him around. I was so enmeshed in my own thoughts, I hardly heard the woman arguing with the trainer about her miserable marriage and how it was all her husband's fault. I was thinking, "Queer how strong those old feelings still are; I almost feel like gagging right now…."

When the tall red-headed professor stood up, I again began to listen. He had spoken earlier, very sensibly too. Maybe he would shed some light on all of this. "I can see," he said, "how I'm responsible for breaking my leg; I was skiing too fast. But I'll be damned if I'm responsible for my car being hit by the drunk who ran the red light." I nodded in agreement.

"We might discuss who put you in that car, on that road, at that particular moment," answered the trainer. "However, it is irrelevant what you think about it, or whether or not you, or any of the rest of you, believe what I'm saying is true. During the coming week, notice what happens when you choose to be responsible—to be 'cause in the matter'—and what happens when you don't."

As we were leaving the room for the dinner break, Andy took my arm. "I like what the trainer said about responsibility."

"What did he say?"

"He said that the degree to which I take responsibility for my life is the degree to which I am the master of it." Arm in arm we crossed the lobby. Andy continued talking. "I definitely am going to use what he said as an operating principle and see what happens this week... I've been thinking about 'complaining.' It looks to me as if every complaint marks a place where I haven't been responsible."

"Oh," I responded vaguely. I was tired of all this talk about responsibility. In my opinion, "being cause in the matter" and "taking responsibility for my life" was gobbledygook. I let go of Andy's arm and pushed through the hotel's heavy swinging door. An image from *As You Like It* darted into my mind—of the world being a stage and I the player. Whereupon I entertained the notion that I must also be the audience... and the author of the play in which I was acting, as well as of these thoughts and the accompanying grim feelings.

On Monday I brooded the entire day. It was as if I had this thing in my hand (called being-wholly-responsible-for-my-life) which I was trying to get rid of. No matter how hard and far I threw it, it always came back to me like a boomerang. What I wanted to do, if the truth were told, was to throw myself on the floor and hold my breath until I turned blue. Then some big Mommie would appear beside me and say, "There, there, I didn't really mean it," and I would crawl into her lap.

Tuesday I said to myself rather smugly, "I'm willing to be responsible for the divorce... but of course Bill has to be, too." Fifty-fifty is how I saw it. But Bill was not willing, and this rankled. How unreasonable of him, how unfair! "But you're the one who left," he countered, "I was perfectly content."

On Wednesday I was having lunch with an old friend from New York. "What happened to your marriage with Bill?" she asked me. "You looked like the perfect couple."

I stirred my omelette around for a minute with my fork. "Well," I finally answered, "imagine a Grand Ball. I have on a long sparkling dress with a wide skirt. The orchestra is playing a waltz, my foot is tapping, and Bill appears before me, bows slightly and, with a divine smile, says 'Want to dance?'

" 'Sure,' I answer eagerly, 'I'd love to.' So we set out, step-close-step, step-close-step across the ballroom floor. Soon I am muttering to myself, 'Oh I do wish he'd take bigger steps... and turn more... turn much, much more, and faster so my skirt can swirl.' After a while I say outloud, 'Gosh, I'm so sorry, but something is wrong with my shoe. My foot hurts horribly. Let's sit down.' And inside I'm grumpy and restless because I really do want to dance. If only he danced right, then I...."

I stopped. I put my fork down and looked at my friend with a sheepish smile. I was feeling slightly dizzy. "Are you all right?" she asked.

"Something just fell into place." I told her about the sentence I had been given: If only he/she would _____, then I would _____. My friend nodded and leaned back in her chair. "You know, I also mutter those kinds of things when Rob and I are dancing. And when we're making love too... especially when we're making love." We looked at each other and laughed, blushing slightly. "Of course, we never say anything about this to them, do we?" she concluded. "We carefully keep our complaints to ourselves."

Thursday morning I wrote to Bill:

> ...When I accused you of holding yourself back, it was I who held back—by not receiving what you were giving me. I feel sad about this... and ask your forgiveness. Thank you for our years together. They richly adorn my life. I love you.

Once I saw that the things I accused Bill of were the very things that I was doing to him, it was absurd to want him to admit to being partly responsible for the divorce. Besides, it was not his job to dance the way I wanted him to. Now, looking at our relationship, I saw it as all right, both the past of it, and the present. I felt whole, like a red apple with no bites out.

In addition to corroding my relationship with Bill, those old leftover resentments cluttered up my relationship with Andy. It was as if we were living in a room jammed with ghostly furniture which I kept bumping into but not seeing. After writing to Bill, most of the furniture had vanished so I could move around more easily. Why, Friday I crossed the room and sat beside Andy without bumping into hardly a thing!

Saturday my friend Sue and I were talking on the telephone about our respective close relationships. Actually, we were talking about our husbands. "Yeah...obviously it's a two-way street," Sue said. "But we conveniently forget we're responsible for both directions.*

*See Disagreeable Truth No. 6 in Appendix II.

Several days later I said to Andy, "Your wrench was on the couch. I moved it to your desk."

"Is that a complaint?" he asked, lifting an eyebrow.

Startled, I opened my eyes wide and then frowned. "Complaint? Of course not! I'm just giving you a useful piece of information." But I had heard the tone of my voice.

That evening I sat on the porch and watched the day end in a glorious suffusion of apricot which reached way over my head. It turned orange and then contracted into a scarlet band above the low western mountains. I heard a covey of quail gabbling softly beyond my garden. Then all was quiet.

"Pity you missed the sunset," I casually remarked to Andy as he came in for a late dinner. I was setting the table.

"That sounds like a complaint to me," he commented with an infuriating smile. I ruffled my feathers in preparation for a vehement denial, and then held my tongue.

When I was cutting the pot-roast I said, in a small voice, "You're right… 'Pity you missed the sunset' was followed inside my head by," and my voice grew louder, "'How come you weren't here to watch it with me'!" I plunked the plates onto the table and sat down. After a few mouthfuls of meat I added, "You know, if you hadn't said anything, I would never have noticed my complaint, I had it so thoroughly concealed. Thanks."

"You're welcome."

"Of course, I never asked you to be home by sunset. Actually, I wasn't even aware that I did want you home by sunset. I'm amazed at how reluctant I am to find out what I want at times. Safer that way, I suppose, then I can just complain covertly and don't have to see all the different places where I refuse to be responsible. What a drag."

Later, when we were getting ready for bed, Andy suggested, "Tomorrow let's play a game. You tell me your complaints and I'll just listen."

I gulped. "Me… complain all day? We'll be at each other's throat before lunch." I hung up my clothes neatly. "I don't like people who complain… such an awful sound. I once had a dream. I was leaving a theatre late at night and I had this whiny, snivelly, white grub of a baby in my arms. I stuffed it under a back-row seat when nobody was looking. That's what I want to do with every complainer."

"Hmmmm," said Andy, hanging up his clothes.

I finished brushing my teeth. "Okay, I'll play."

The next morning I was the first out of bed. As I reached for my bathrobe, my first complaint was at hand. "You put your bathrobe on top of mine! You're so… so messy." My second complaint came ten minutes later, in the kitchen. "You forgot to empty the dishpan last night. It's full of cold greasy water." In fifteen minutes up popped my third. "I found your coffee cup on your desk and the residue is stuck on the bottom." "How can you waste so much time on the phone?" was my fourth. They went on and on. I felt like a batter with a box of balls beside me. All day I kept hitting complaints like flies to Andy, who just kept catching them.

At last we sat down and recounted what we had noticed—where it had been especially hard, where especially uncomfortable, what we had liked and not liked, where we had been angry or frustrated or had laughed. I was sitting cross-legged on the couch, leaning forward and waving my hands as I talked. Andy had pulled up a chair to face me. His eyes were very blue and bright; when he talked, his head moved. Then there was a pause and we both stretched. "Do you think our relationship has suffered?" Andy asked in mock mournful tones.

"No," I answered. "But it could have!" and I smiled. When I looked, I had to agree that the ineffable subtance called "quality" had increased. So obviously, the content of one's remarks is not what counts. We had just demonstrated to ourselves that observing is the source of quality in our relationship.

12. Commitment
[Latin: to join, to put together]

It was windy. As I walked along the ridge, long tawny grasses bent
and swept the ground, scraggly bushes shook their branches, the
mesquite leaves looked like wriggling worms. All around, my calm,
still desert was jiggling and I disliked the wind fingering my clothes.
I turned my eyes westward and let them slide down the gently falling
land to the distant plain where dust devils swirled two thousand feet
below. After a moment I brought my eyes back to my feet and the path,
and continued chewing on the word "commit." I had been doing this for
several hours.

Walking along, I remembered the first time I heard Peter cry. He was hungry, and though I wanted to sleep, I—a proud nursing mother—was the source of his breakfast. As I clambered reluctantly out of bed, I knew in my bones what commitment was. Peter was in my life irrevocably and forever. It did not matter what I wanted, did not want, or what I thought about it. His well-being would always bear on mine. It is natural to care for what I feel joined with, beginning with my body and moving out to include my children.

After a while two ravens flew by, gurgling back and forth. Just beyond me they began to circle higher and higher, and then they swung on the wind in great intersecting loops, still talking. I wanted to call to them, "Hey you! What's it like up there?"

Soon they stopped their aerial acrobatics and, side by side, passed low over my head with a swish of feathers, cawing a few times. They dipped below the crest of a hill so I no longer could see them, but they left me with the queer feeling that somehow we were all in this together, every last one of us, since the moment we were born.

Back at the house I ate a sandwich and then decided to clean out my studio desk. In a bottom drawer I found a colored photograph of a luminous round pebble mottled with swirls of blue, brown and white. The photo had been taken by an astronaut and he called it The Place Where We All Live. To an astronaut, glancing over his shoulder at the spinning ball from whence he came, it must be obvious that to have been put on that ball is to be joined together, is to be committed. I am sure all of us when very young had a sense of being connected. But as with other things, we forget. We become afraid, build protecting walls, and instead of feeling safe, we feel even more afraid. How odd we must appear to the old-man-in-the-moon.

Looking at the photograph, I remembered my own fear—that of loosing my "Ann-ness"—which I use to define my specialness and to maintain my sense of personal existence. Every so often this fear surges in to pound on the shores of my being. I found four thumbtacks and fastened the photograph to the left of my desk as a reminder of where I live.

When I left my studio, sunlight glanced off of one of Joe's mirrors embedded around the fence posts. It caught my eye. Joe was right; those pieces of mirror occasionally do surprise me.

Most of my life I have confined my sense of being interrelated to my immediate family and a few select friends. That was as far as I would demonstrate my concern. The ranch community presented the actuality of kinship with those whom I considered "not my type." Gradually I extended my notions of family even farther, so that when I volunteered for a service organization, I could recognize I was committed to those whom I called strangers. The feeling of being connected to them was the same as the feeling of being connected to my children, or to the ravens. More than that, now came the possibility of caring for a person's well-being whom I might not like.

Often I add so much significance to the word "commitment" that I perversely disregard I am continually manifesting it as naturally as I breathe. (Occasionally I may even do this by being committed to the point of view that I am not committed.) Choosing the job of ranch secretary was one of the ways I made my underlying sense of connectedness visible to myself. This changed how I related to our community; all of it became "my house."

Another way was by saying to Andy before family and friends, "I take thee." For months I resisted stepping again into marriage. Looking back, I can see that a lie blocked the way. I would not admit that I had violated my commitment to my first husband. I did this not by leaving him, but by claiming that I had not ever really committed myself to him. "When I married Bill, I was much too young to know what I was saying," is how I tried to excuse myself.

One of the questions in my current lexicon is, "To what am I committed right now?" Out of viewing the ranch as my house, when something needs to be done (like turning on the well), I will look around, and if no one is there to step forward, I do it. I might even step forward without first looking around—unless I am upset and so engrossed in criticizing the person who was supposed to turn on the well that I lose touch with my prior commitment to the efficient operation of the ranch. I will then scurry off to find that person without first turning on the well.

In my relationship with Andy, I am committed to his well-being. But when I am angry I may temporarily be committed to punishing him (as I have described in earlier pages). It is the seeing of this that begins to unravel my anger.

13. To Choose

    Several months ago at breakfast, Andy was talking about his relationship with his daughter Maggie, who is adopted. "There is nothing that binds me to her but the fact that I went to Phoenix and chose her. The boys just happened to me...." He sipped his coffee reflectively for a few moments and then continued. "No matter how angry I get with her, I just can't say 'to hell with it,' and take her back to Phoenix... although when I'm really upset, I'd like to. So in a way I have to choose her again and again... Freedom is continually being the author of choice."

    "Yes, I see what you're saying. It's another of those awful truths... choosing never being over." I sighed. "I do so much want to have done with something, and then put it safely away in the cupboard along with my jars of tomatoes."

"That's called 'death'," said Andy chuckling. I smiled back ruefully.

Choosing is not a favorite activity. You know how it is sometimes. We shuffle around in the vestibule asking ourselves, "Is this the right door?…Or this one over here?…Or maybe that one would be better?" We are so preoccupied with the dilemma of making the correct choice, we hardly have the time to eat or sleep. Once we have chosen, we breathe a secret sigh of relief and step out into the world again and get on with our lives.

However the moment I have finally declared "I'll take this one!" (whether a person, a job, or No. 4 on the menu), my mosquito voice begins buzzing, trying to prove that "You have made a dreadful mistake this time, stupid. You should have chosen the other one."

Over the breakfast dishes, I thought of the day I stood before family and friends, looked at Andy and said, "I take thee." I felt as if I were jumping off a high cliff; our entire acquaintance flashed by with all the things I did not like about him specially magnified. By marrying him I was saying "yes" to those things as well as to what I liked. Saying "yes" to them is, in a sense, choosing them. This is quite different from tolerating them, or enduring them, which is what I usually do. I experience little satisfaction that way. Choosing is a creative act.

A few days later, I asked my son Michael if I could go camping with him the next time he went, and he said, "Sure." The following week we set out. When Michael started to light the evening's first fire, I was about to go over and take the kindling out of his hands with a motherly, "Here, let me do it." (A sneaky way of saying, "You're not doing it right.") Then I remembered I had asked Michael to let me go with him, and I sat down. Asking to go along is accepting (from the Latin root 'to take') his way of doing things, like the way he makes fires. At that moment I actually chose him, all of him, even his habit of burying his head in a book and not answering when I spoke to him, even the way he wore his hair (which I had magnanimously been putting up with… and the choosing of which also included my not liking it, and not liking that I did not like it, etc. etc.) I took a deep breath. Suddenly everything around me snapped into focus. My breath relaxed. As I watched Michael light the fire, I saw his competence and inventiveness. A few minutes later he handed me a perfectly chilled glass of Chablis with an elegant flourish and a smile that brought tears to my eyes. I fell in love with him, just as I had on the day he was born. I heard a coyote yap far away and closer at hand, the crackle of the fire.

14. Contract
[Latin: to draw together]

One evening during the last Christmas holidays, when three of Andy's children were home from college, Sam suggested a poker game. "Do you want to play, Ann?"

"Sure, count me in."

At the conclusion of the fourth hand, I claimed a Straight beat a Flush. Sam took the book of rules from the shelf. I lost. I hated losing that hand so much, I wanted to pick up my chips and leave. Yet I knew that without rules there is no game. A contract, that is, a set of rules or agreements, spells out clearly a particular game's procedure; commitment provides the framework in which to play the game. In fact, until the commitment is declared with a "Count me in," or "I take thee," there is no game. A declaration, made visible by a contract, harnesses one's mind and defangs such thoughts as "I don't like it so I'm quitting!" Such thoughts, if acted upon, end the game. If I responded to these, I would be packing my bag at least once a week. Really.

Once Andy and I had declared our commitment to each other, in the form of marriage, we decided to draw up a set of agreements. This is helpful in the game of relationship, especially when a relationship is physically close, like boss and secretary, mother and child, room-mates, etc. Working out our contract was an exercise for me in seeing what I thought I wanted, did not want, what my expectations were, and my fears. It took us days to boil down our agreements to the essentials.* I highly recommend the process; I found it very valuable. Then we promised to keep our agreements, the keeping of which we faced daily.

*See Appendix IV.

Our contract is renegotiable; our commitment is not, nor is it revocable. Commitment is a different order of things. Yet by means of our contract, we can from time to time change the form in which our relationship expresses itself.

A word of warning about hidden rules and agreements: They operate surreptitiously behind the scene and are insidious. Sooner or later, in my close relationships, they cause mischief. For example, one hot summer morning I came into the kitchen and was assailed by a powerful odor. "Perhaps a mouse has died," I said to myself, sniffing here and there. Finally, I tracked it to the garbage can under the sink and remembered the chicken bones I had thrown away a few days before. At that moment Andy walked into the kitchen. I said to him angrily, "Say, the garbage is stinking. How come you didn't empty it when you were supposed to."

"What do you mean—'When you're supposed to'?"

After a short debate, I finally realized we never had a rule about garbage. Andy had been removing it regularly and I was taking his doing it for granted. In addition, I took it so for granted I never thanked him.

"In some ways," said Andy, "tacit agreements are as much of an agreement as openly expressed ones. I certainly lent myself to this one." He went over to the sink, picked up the garbage can and went out the door.

Yesterday, Andy and I agreed to meet at 4:15 outside the bank. I promised to be on time, and I was ten minutes late. "So sorry," I said breathlessly as I rushed up to him. "I had to get some gas…and…and I think my clock is slow." Andy gave me a cold fishy stare. Ignoring it, I hurried on. "It was only a few minutes…you were later than that to dinner the other night!" Then I heard my words; and laughed. Sometimes I hate admitting I have broken a promise. Admitting it is the first essential step in sweeping up the pieces.

Sometimes I pretend broken promises do not matter. But each is a pebble in my shoe, and a pebble in my shoe has consequences. You know how it is when you cannot count on somebody's word…when they never are there when they said they would be. This affects how I deal with them as well as affecting the quality of our relationship.

And sometimes certain promises and agreements just do not work. They need to be revised or rescinded. However you do want to keep them long enough so as to give them a fair test and not back out at the first twinges of discomfort or thoughts of "I don't want to."

Such a one for me was my promise to myself to run down to the fence every day in my commitment to stay physically fit. One Monday it was cold and windy so I did not run, saying to myself, "I'm sure running in this icy wind is bad for me." One Thursday I did not run because I though I was getting a blister. (Of course I went dancing that night.) Another time I was too busy to run, not too busy to talk with my friends, however. Etc. etc. Instead of accomplishing my daily run, I had a fine collection of reasons why I was not accomplishing my daily run. Eventually I had to admit I was breaking my word.

The truth was that I found running to be very uncomfortable; my knees hurt. So I discovered I was committed to my comfort rather than to my physical fitness. I began to notice where else I broke a promise because I refused to be uncomfortable. Broken promises very neatly sort out and reveal that which controls me. As odd as it sounds, they are valuable. They point to what I am really committed to, which has been hidden underneath what I think or believe I am committed to. Subsequently I found a form of exercise which suited me and would keep me physically fit. Then I remade my promise and told it to Andy. Declaring a promise acts like the keel of a ship; it helps to keep me on course and upright during the buffetings of a storm.

15. Goals and Purpose

Everyone has goals.

"Not me!" I silently reassured myself the first time I heard this statement. At that time I thought badly of goals. They were fine for racehorses, and possibly generals, but on the whole they were what was wrong with our country. We were far too goal-oriented. And I refused to see that wanting my children to be happy was a goal; expecting Andy to take a walk with me was a goal; cooking a very good dinner was a goal. Goals are what get me out of bed in the morning. My life is paved with them, and so is yours.

In my family goals were never mentioned. Somehow they were connected with ambition and sweat, so of course ladies pretended not to have them. "Whatever you say, dear," my grandmother would assure my father, or my uncle, or Gramps, smiling and fluttering her eyelashes ever so slightly. "Anything you want, dear." But I knew she got exactly what she wanted. I was not surprised that afterwards those around her looked grumpy, but I was puzzled that afterwards her mouth turned down.

One Sunday morning my secret goal was to show off my big leghorn hat and new blue dress to the boy behind the counter at Scott's drugstore. So I had to "persuade" my mother to stop there after church. She wanted to hurry home and listen to the opera. Hardly had the car doors slammed shut than I started to work on her. "Do let's stop at Scott's. I need some paper for school tomorrow."

"I have some you can have, dear."

"It has to be lined, and just the right size... It's only a few blocks out of the way."

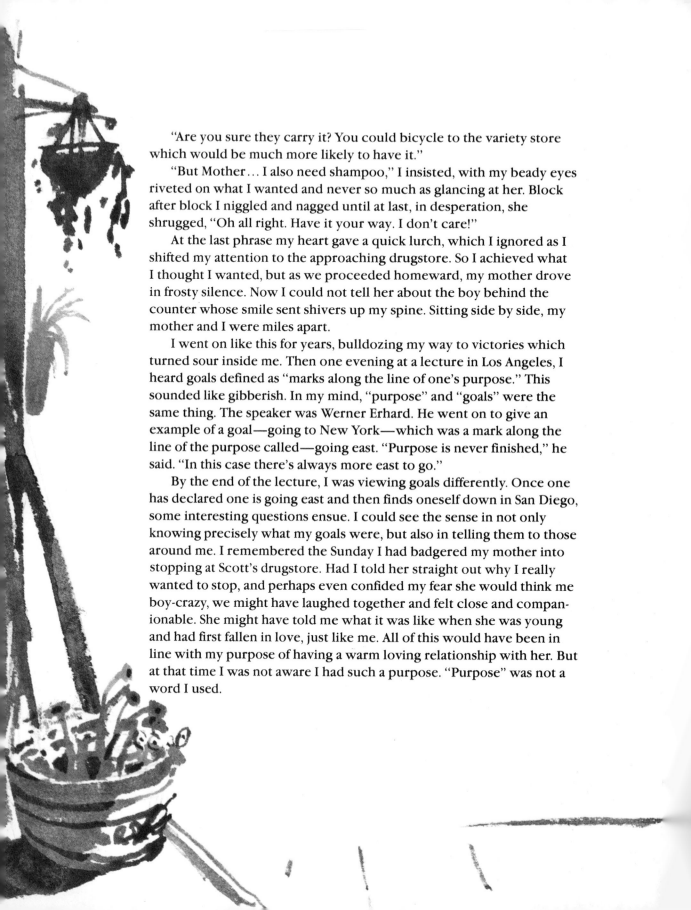

"Are you sure they carry it? You could bicycle to the variety store which would be much more likely to have it."

"But Mother... I also need shampoo," I insisted, with my beady eyes riveted on what I wanted and never so much as glancing at her. Block after block I niggled and nagged until at last, in desperation, she shrugged, "Oh all right. Have it your way. I don't care!"

At the last phrase my heart gave a quick lurch, which I ignored as I shifted my attention to the approaching drugstore. So I achieved what I thought I wanted, but as we proceeded homeward, my mother drove in frosty silence. Now I could not tell her about the boy behind the counter whose smile sent shivers up my spine. Sitting side by side, my mother and I were miles apart.

I went on like this for years, bulldozing my way to victories which turned sour inside me. Then one evening at a lecture in Los Angeles, I heard goals defined as "marks along the line of one's purpose." This sounded like gibberish. In my mind, "purpose" and "goals" were the same thing. The speaker was Werner Erhard. He went on to give an example of a goal—going to New York—which was a mark along the line of the purpose called—going east. "Purpose is never finished," he said. "In this case there's always more east to go."

By the end of the lecture, I was viewing goals differently. Once one has declared one is going east and then finds oneself down in San Diego, some interesting questions ensue. I could see the sense in not only knowing precisely what my goals were, but also in telling them to those around me. I remembered the Sunday I had badgered my mother into stopping at Scott's drugstore. Had I told her straight out why I really wanted to stop, and perhaps even confided my fear she would think me boy-crazy, we might have laughed together and felt close and companionable. She might have told me what it was like when she was young and had first fallen in love, just like me. All of this would have been in line with my purpose of having a warm loving relationship with her. But at that time I was not aware I had such a purpose. "Purpose" was not a word I used.

One of the things that keeps me denying I have goals, is my fear of failure. Besides meaning that I am deficient, incompetent, no good, etc., my failure to reach a goal is unendurably embarrassing. So I pretend I am not really trying to reach such-and-such, I am merely out for a stroll. And thus I cheat myself because my failure to reach a goal is a signpost inscribed with information which I will not see when I am pretending not to have a goal. Nor will I see it when I am busily scolding myself or blaming others for my lack of success.

I hasten to add that success is as rich a source of information as failure. Just as our attitudes about failure blind us to this information, so too do our attitudes about success. The more clearly and specifically we state our goals, the more useful the information they provide, whether or not we attain them.

Writing this book has been an exercise in setting goals. One day I said, "By 6 p.m. Friday I will finish writing about responsibility." Then Friday ended and I had not finished. "Oh," I concluded, "I did not plan well enough." I had put too many items on that week's calendar. The third time I failed to reach my target of finishing "responsibility," the underlying truth was inescapable: I had little enthusiasm for the subject. Actually, I wanted to sweep it under the rug.

In a close relationship, I had better recognize that I and the other person have goals, whether spoken or not. There is nothing wrong with keeping them to myself, but I had better know that I run the risk of my behavior appearing puzzling or obscure. Without a doubt, hiding my goals from my mother threw sand into the gears of our relationship. At that time this was exactly what I thought I wanted to do, in order to punish her for some fancied grievance. (I call that "cutting off one's nose to spite one's face.")

Telling Andy my goals makes it possible for him to encourage and sustain me when my interest flags. I do not always spontaneously welcome this, I fear, but in the end I profit from it.

The dishes are washed, the floor is swept, my bills are paid and I am alone in the house with a long quiet afternoon stretching before me, only it is slightly marred by Aspect No. 3. I have finally decided to tackle it; I open my canary yellow notebook and begin to read.

June 5. Andy came up with a third aspect: A relationship is expanded by a purpose larger than its own continuance. He presented it to me at breakfast. It rang in my ears like a long clear note wrested from a dream. Immediately I wanted to protest, to brush it aside. Too late, it already had slipped through my carefully tended jungle of words and struck my heart, sending out tiny tremulous ripples to the tips of my fingers.

I put my hand on the page and gaze out the window. A neat brown bird is hopping along a branch looking for bugs. How shiny the oak leaves are today, and with so many little blue spaces in between. I turn the page.

June 12. My cousin called last night. He's all in a stew about his girl friend. "We spend hours and hours talking about our relationship. We really are working hard on it, but it feels like glue." Andy cocked an eyebrow when I repeated this to him. "No wonder," he said, "when you're constantly sifting through your garbage...."

October 22. "Even when I was very young, I knew my life had a larger purpose than myself and my problems," said Andy at lunch today. "Deep in my heart I had a destinal resolve." The last two words sounded like a bell tolling. "That's because you were an altar boy," I answered irritably... What I remembered was wanting to be Mowgli safely hidden in the jungle with my animal friends and peering out unseen through the flickering leaves at the grownups, the enemy. I also wanted to be Peter Pan.

November 1. Behind the mops and brooms in a Tucson market I came upon a friend I haven't seen since moving to the ranch . She invited me to lunch. "I'd like to ask you something," Nancy said, settling herself on the other side of the small table. "I just finished reading your book about your boys and all those crazy animals. You sounded like you were having a great time. I can't figure out why you and Bill were divorced."

I fiddled with my dark glasses and shrugged. "I've explained it to myself in different ways at different times. You had children. You know how it is. Your children take off and there you are, the two of you, with nothing to do together. Looking back, I can see that outside of raising the boys, my sense of purpose was entirely derived from Bill's public service job. As his wife, I felt I also had a useful role. Then when he resigned to work on a personal project and my job with the boys was essentially done, there I was... feeling like a rudderless boat wallowing aimlessly about. I had no sense of purpose anymore, not for myself and not for our relationship. I was expecting Bill to somehow give this to me."

"I know exactly what you're saying. I've decided to take my State Bar exams and I'm hoping Jack and I can be partners."

"What I did was to move to the ranch and marry Andy."

"Yeah... I remember being shocked. And fascinated."

"Then Andy and I did the *est* Training, which for me opened up the whole question of purpose. First I had to admit that I had been deliberately keeping myself in the dark about it, especially since obviously a purpose has to be noble... and grand... like selling your worldly goods and going off to India tightly laced in whalebone... to feed the starving. Lots of gold stars on your report card, but no fun."

"I think that way too," Nancy agreed. "Definitely feeding the starving counts, but not keeping house."

"Oh but it might, if you were keeping house for someone who was feeding the starving." I went on to tell her about Aspect No. 3: "If a close relationship doesn't have a purpose larger than its own survival, it will continue, but it will gradually become pale and thin, just as mine with Bill did. After the Training, I could see I was entirely responsible for this happening. And what kept me from engaging myself with the issue was my firmly held conviction that purpose meant Sacrifice. I might not get what I wanted—as well as having to give up what I already had."

Nancy laughed. "So you too keep such boogeymen in your closet to scare yourself with."

November 10. By now I can easily see the benefits I derive from keeping this particular boogeyman of mine around. Like, not being tempted to take on something I might not like or might fail at. As for the price-tag? Maybe tomorrow I'll look at that.

I turn a few pages and pause at a letter from Carol, a college classmate. She began it by telling me about an interview she had read in the newspaper with an American. He had just been released after years of solitary confinement in a Chinese prison.

November 21. ...For the first few months (she wrote) he had been overwhelmed with despair. Yet as awful as it was to have lost family, friends, music, etc., he realized the one thing that made his life worth living was the sense of making a contribution to the 'long river of human progress.' Since this was a matter of quality not scale as he had always thought, he could actually do it even when in solitary confinement. He kept his cell spotless with bits of rag and was attentive to every interchange with his guards. But each morning on waking up he had to remind himself that *he was capable* of making a contribution *exactly where he was....*

Quite a story isn't it? I could profit by such a thought when I climb out of bed. If he can look upon all those years in prison as an addition to his life...then what about all the things I consider to be a waste of time...*

Yesterday (I had written on the back of her letter) I showed Carol's letter to Andy. After a silence he said, "How clearly the man demonstrates that a purpose is invented and kept alive by oneself. Though it is imagined, one must treat it as if it were real."

Again I look out the window. A wind has come up. The blue spaces between the oak leaves tirelessly change their shapes. I think about my boogeyman called "Purpose as Sacrifice." It still lives in my closet; when it pops out I wave to it and wink.

*See Disagreeable Truth No. 7 in Appendix II.

"How does Aspect no. 3 affect your relationship with Andy," my mother asked me during her last visit. She had been reading the first few chapters of this book. "In ordinary practical terms," I answered, "one thing is that I don't complain about his evening meetings. From the point of view of this Aspect, I see them differently. I recognize that he is attending to other facets of life for me. Believe me, I thank him!... I am continually amazed at how nourishing our relationship is, even when it's uncomfortable. And sometimes it looks like an unending mess of problems.   Come to think of it, our relationship sure is a great launching platform—out into the world."

Recently Andy went east on a business trip and to visit two of his sons. He planned a day of canoeing with them on a nearby river. He called me at the end of their visit and I asked how the canoeing had gone. "We didn't," he answered. "It rained all day. I was very disappointed and was settling down to have a miserable time. Then I asked myself what was my purpose in being here. And it wasn't canoeing! What I cared about was being with the kids. That was my purpose. So we had a great time eating hamburgers and going to a movie."

Several times since then, when things did not seem to be going the way I thought I wanted them to, I have asked myself, "What is my purpose?" This question nudges me away from the fascinating whirlpool of disaster and I begin to see the situation less as a predicament and more as an opportunity.

Here at the ranch our spirit of cooperation took on a new dimension when we incorporated and formally declared that this community had a purpose, namely: to provide an environment conducive to artistic and related endeavors. I noticed that I felt differently about the endless roof-fixing, the plumbing and electrical emergencies, the disagreements and fights. Our problems became simply steps in the carrying out of our attested purpose as a community. It probably would not matter what our purpose is, as long as we have taken it to heart. Those moments when I am seized by the thought that living here is a very bad idea indeed, and the time has come to move on, I remember that deep in my heart I have pledged myself to having this community function in the light of its purpose. Without that perhaps each of us would have drifted off to where living seemed easier.

Periodically, here at the ranch, we join together to paint a roof, re-stucco a wall, fix a road, clean up the gallery. I am likely to give those who did not come to help a black look the next time our paths cross. I have a well-developed opinion about what comprises "keeping up one's end" which, in my book of portraits, is a requirement for staying on the team. Joining a work party counts; producing a drawing does not count. Living on the ranch is a continual practice for me in broadening my notions of what it is to make a contribution to the team.

Our having declared a community purpose, and my personally aligning myself with it, made some new things visible in my close relationships. When Andy and I moved from the big white U-shaped house into the one where we now live (still on the ranch), we disagreed noisily as to how the furniture should be arranged in the living room. I wanted the couch against the east wall; he wanted it against the south wall. He wanted the piano to the left of one door; I wanted it to the right of another door, and we each marshalled up our reasons to prove that our way was right. The day was hot. We were hot. And it crossed my mind several times that Andy should have remained in the other house. Finally we pushed a few boxes of books aside and sat down in the middle of the floor. Given that we clearly understood and were aligned with the purpose of our relationship, we could spell out precisely what our living room had to accomplish. Once we did this, we saw precisely where to put the piano and the couch.

When we were last in Guadalajara, we spent an afternoon in an old cemetery overgrown and tangled. Bees hummed there in the hot sunlight. In the shadows the air was faintly tinged with jasmine. Andy painted a picture under a rose arbor and pale pink petals came to rest on his paper. I wandered among the tombstones.

A worn grey one caught my eye. It was tilted and partly lifted out of the ground by the roots of an enormous fig tree which embraced it. With some difficulty I finally deciphered part of the inscription.

> Donna Isabella.........am...
> 179.........
> Long before death.........
> She set us free.
> Sus Hijos

"Not a bad epitaph," I said to myself. Over a shrimp dinner in a small neighborhood cantina, I told Andy what Donna Isabella's children had said about her. We each decided to compose an epitaph for ourselves. While I ate shrimp, thought and mumbled, Andy took out his pen and on a clean paper napkin decisively wrote: "He served God." By the time the dessert arrived, I had finally extracted from my scribblings: "She was a great innkeeper."

"What made you a great innkeeper?" Andy asked.

"The fact that travellers arrived frazzled and left refreshed and able to easily climb the mountains ahead." Later I put this more grandly: "She returned them to themselves."

Occasionally we will ask our friends, were they to have a tombstone, what they would like it to proclaim. "What I am here for," said one of these friends, "and I quote from the Scottish Shorter Catechism, is 'to glorify God and enjoy Him forever'." I like that.

16. To Serve

I have a reproduction of an old Japanese woodcut fastened to the inside of my studio door. An aunt, travelling in the Orient, sent it to me on the occasion of the birth of my youngest son, Hugh. It depicts an elegantly coifed woman with her head demurely bent. In her hands she holds a tea cup and saucer which, as I see it, she is ready to place before a gentleman. She imparts waiting, waiting to serve.

When I first looked at the woodcut I was extremely irritated, so irritated in fact that I put the picture in a drawer. It remained there for years, but every so often I would think of that woman and be annoyed all over again. "Boy, what a simp, what a doormat!" I would say to myself. "Hey, lady, you'll never get anywhere that way. Lift your head...step out. He can fetch his own cup of tea."

Underneath the woodcut is a quote from the Ramayana given to me by Joe. He wrote it in calligraphy on sky blue paper.

When I don't know who I am, I serve you.
When I know who I am, I am you.

After Joe had thumbtacked the quote on my studio door, I received a letter from a friend in Somalia about the work he was doing in a refugee camp and I remembered something Albert Schweitzer said—how we will be truly happy when we have sought and found how to serve. "Service" was suddenly blazoned across my eyes and I had to finally admit that I had long been avoiding that word. Like "purpose," it too meant sacrifice; it meant my having to do what someone else wanted rather than what I wanted.

My rambles through the landscape of relationship have revealed journeys within journeys, and each has a question for a guiding light. (By the way, every time we answer it, the light goes out and only goes on again when we re-ask the question.)

"What is it to serve?" is the question belonging to a journey which began with my angry reaction to the woodcut. Joe's quote lies off in the distance—a shimmering lake I occasionally glimpse through the trees. The more I resist its pull, the more I am aware of its presence.*

Tuesday afternoon I returned to the house looking forward to a hot shower and an hour with a new spy story. Andy was in the kitchen making himself a peanut butter sandwich. "What perfect timing," he called to me. "I was about to go find someone to give me a hand with the well. The job shouldn't take more than half an hour. Will you come?" Going with him was serving. It was doing what needed to be done right then. Sometimes my commitment to what needs to be done is at my finger tips and I respond immediately and wholeheartedly. Other times I go into a spasm of resistance, of "I don't want to." And this introduces the word "surrender," which for me often is the doorway to serving.

Every one of us somewhere in our life, and in some form, has stumbled onto the ancient paradox: In surrendering oneself one finds one's self. It may be while skiing, or during childbirth or sex, or while walking down a crowded street. "Or drawing," said Andy. "Or working out a problem," said Hugh, now a mathematician. In surrendering to what I think is not at all what I want, to what appears to be unacceptably different from myself, I discover I am *that* too.

*See Disagreeable Truth No. 8 in Appendix II.

Today is the first day of spring. Crossing the living room, my eyes rest on a windowpane. In the glass I see my face, and through the glass I see Andy, who is outside sitting on a bench doing a watercolor of purple iris. In the glass, my eyes are just above his head, and I am smiling. I step out the door and sit beside him.

Silently I watch the iris grow on his paper. Our shoulders touch briefly as he changes position. "The hummingbirds have been fighting over the sugar water," he says, adding a touch of blue to a petal.

Over our heads clouds are passing, great solitary islands flat-bottomed and edged with light. They slide by on an invisible sea, on their way to some secret rendezvous no doubt, way beyond the town of Oracle. I watch the clouds to the south trailing shadows across the mountains on the other side of which I once lived. "The radio says it will rain tomorrow."

"Wouldn't be surprised. There's moisture in the air…makes the paper different," says Andy. I watch green grow into a leaf. The cat comes around the corner and settles at our feet. I reach down and scratch behind his ears. He leans into my fingers.

Then the cat begins to grow on Andy's paper next to the iris. I return inside to cook our dinner. Closing the door, I again catch sight of my face in the windowpane and look through it to Andy just beyond. I am pleased with our blending.